How to Sell Your Business
—and get what you want!

How to Sell Your Business
—and get what you want!

A Pragmatic Guide
with *Revealing* Tips
from 57 Sellers

Colin Gabriel

Gwent Press Inc., Westport, Connecticut

First Edition

Gwent Press Inc. 14 Darbrook Road Westport, Connecticut 06880

Printed in the United States of America

Book design by Toshiko Gabriel

This book is intended to provide information, but it is no substitute for appropriate legal, accounting, and other professional guidance. Every effort has been made to make this book accurate, but it may contain mistakes, and certain rules and regulations are subject to change.

The purpose of this book is to identify issues for further study, and for review with professional advisors. Neither the author nor the publisher shall have liability or responsibility to any person or entity concerning any loss or damage caused, or alleged to be caused, directly or indirectly, by the information contained in this book.

Return this book to the publisher for a full refund if you do not wish to be bound by the above disclaimer.

Publisher's Cataloging-in-Publication
(*provided by Quality Books, Inc.*)

Gabriel, Colin
How to sell your business—and get what you want!: a pragmatic guide with tips from 57 sellers/Colin Gabriel—1st ed.
p. cm.
Includes index.
Preassigned LCCN: 97-92965
ISBN: 0-9656578-3-3

1. Sale of business enterprises. I. Title

HD1393.25.G33 1998 658.1'6
QBI97-40504

---

9 8 7 6 5 4 3 2 1

Contents

Introduction

First, some pointers:

- **Recognize the imbalance.** Buyers buy regularly; sellers seldom sell more than once. It is not an even match. Prepare accordingly.
- **Look beyond the pitch.** Suitors aim to please. Owners tend to *rule*. Investigate buyers.
- **Be realistic.** Art is auctioned; houses are sold slowly. Most businesses are analogous to houses.
- **Commit to explore**–not to sell. Go slowly before shaking hands on a price.
- **Get ready early.** After an agreement in principle, delay equals risk, and incomplete papers will postpone the closing.
- **Sell *future* profits.** Document these expectations.
- **Assume nothing.** Run the business, right up to the closing, as if it will be yours indefinitely. It might be. Decisions made in anticipation of a closing can be costly.

- ***Invest* in audited statements.** Financial statements assume *huge* importance–more than ever before. They permit you to (1) close faster (less investigation), (2) make fewer, shorter guarantees, and (3) demand more cash at the closing. Audited financial statements make you more nimble. With them you can switch readily among suitors–you may not want to, but buyers will know you *could*. Buyers seek confidence in future performance; past performance, audited, is the best indicator. Higher confidence equals higher price.
- **Understand the financing.** Before signing anything, know the buyer's financing plans. Know the sources of equity, bank debt, or subordinated debt. What will the balance sheet look like after the closing? You should know–but you won't be told unless you ask.
- **Remain on guard.** Competition among buyers is a powerful force to protect you in negotiations: it often breaks down, to the seller's disadvantage, after an agreement in principle is signed.
- **Disclose everything.** Problems uncovered late threaten both the price and the deal itself.
- **Take charge.** Experienced professionals can coach, but *you* must execute. You have the big economic stake, and you, unlike your advisors, may go to work–for years–for the new company. Don't give up the helm.

Part One

What works for one business owner may not work for another. And your style counts. Here, in Part One, are tips from 57 people who sold their businesses for between $2 million and over $100 million. The buyers were public companies, private companies, investors, employees, and foreign companies–and there is a chapter for each category. You should find advice applicable to you in these interviews.

Part Two

Most business sales follow a pattern. I describe the steps in sequence in Part Two, and quote tips from the sellers.

Before Talking

You need insights into the perspective of buyers. Chapter 6 suggests steps you can take to learn more about mergers and acquisitions–read what buyers read, and perhaps socialize with them. (Chapters 1-5 are tips from sellers.)

If you want the best price, be prepared. Chapter 7 reviews what you should consider before talking to a buyer, including recasting financial statements, selling surplus assets, and developing a successor.

Finding the Buyer

Chapter 8 compares reacting to inquiries versus taking the initiative. An inquiry from a qualified buyer can be a tempting lure. Taking the initiative offers a chance to create competition among buyers to boost the price. Declaring a business for sale is risky.

Brokers can introduce buyers you would not find on your own. Chapter 9 discusses the role of brokers, how much they are paid, and how you should control them.

Copy those who seek venture capital–use a business plan to sell your story. Barely legible financial schedules do not instill confidence. Statements bound in the cover of an accounting firm are better. Presentation counts. Chapter 10 is about selling your story.

You might be wary of a buyer wanting to burden your business with debt, but this could be your best deal. Some 200 leveraged buyout firms control over $200 billion in buying power. This is an *enormous* segment of the market. Chapter 11 reviews leveraged buyouts.

Price is the focal point, but it should not overshadow other concerns. Chapter 12 discusses price.

Negotiating the Deal

Negotiations are the subject of Chapter 13. The best weapon is a sound alternative. Momentum is crucial–if the deal is not hurtling towards a closing, it might be in trouble. Chapter 14 discusses letters of intent–at this time you agree on a price, and you agree to take the business off the market for 60 to 90 days. Few sellers appreciate how often buyers withdraw, or change the deal, after this milestone.

Chapter 15 reviews the role of lawyers. When you get a bill for $30,000 for a deal that did not close, you may be sorry you consulted your attorney so early. If, however, you sign a letter of intent without advice from an experienced lawyer, you may have missed your best opportunity to win key points.

Due diligence (the buyer's investigation of your business) is painful–see Chapter 16. It begins immediately after the signing of a letter of intent, and it seldom takes less than 60 days–it can take six months. The time is designated for investigating your business, but a leveraged buyer also uses this time to arrange the financing–and either task can cause delays.

Chapter 17 discusses definitive agreements. With economic issues scattered throughout, these contracts require some give and take.

Sometimes the buyer lowers the price after investigating your business. A bank may have decreed the price too high, or someone somewhere might have suggested you would take less. Now your negotiating skills will be tested–and you will be glad you spent time before signing the letter of intent to learn what others might pay for the business. See Chapter 18.

Life with New Owners

Negotiations continue after the closing–over escrows, employment agreements, and earn-outs. Would you like to buy the business back? The opportunity, discussed in Chapter 19, arises sometimes, and it is often for a fraction of the price you received. Even better, seller-financing may be available.

Resources

Resources are in the Appendix. You will help yourself by tapping pertinent information wherever you can find it. The Internet and online computer services offer a treasure trove. See page 209. The Internet does not eliminate the utility of other services–if you know exactly what you want, and where to find it, the most efficient way to access reams of business information is on services tailored to such use. If, for example, you make medical diagnostic products, you can, at modest expense, set up an account with an online computer service to save all press releases on designated wire services that mention the word "diagnostic." You will get some items of no interest, but you will also see many relevant to your task. The same service can pick up all announcements made by selected companies (domestic and foreign) you are following.

If you are expecting executives from a public company to visit you, you might like to see (online) all the press releases the company issued in the last few years, and find information that otherwise might not be presented to you. You can also search through hundreds of regional and trade newspapers for articles on people and companies–and often find revealing facts (see page 213).

ABI/Inform is a database available via various online services. Here you can find articles by experts from numerous professional journals–on the arcane rules governing the limited use of a net operating loss by a buyer of your business; on strategies like "short-against-the-box" to hedge your position if you are holding restricted stock; and on the rules for a tax-free exchange. See page 215.

Also in the Appendix is "One Story" (page 222), not particularly unusual, of a seller who had agreements in principle with three buyers before concluding a sale to a public company, one that had withdrawn from talks *twice* before consummating the acquisition.

Do-it-yourself is not recommended. One size does not fit all: no worksheets or sample agreements are included.

PART ONE

Tips from Sellers

1

Businesses Sold to Public Companies

All but one of the interviews were conducted on the telephone and taped. I asked each seller what advice he would give a friend about how to sell a business. Negotiations came up in some conversations, as did working for the new owner. I asked most people for their view of the top three issues for a seller. Only the answers are presented here–the questions asked are apparent from the quotations. I was unable to get written consent to quote four of those interviewed, and their answers are attributed to "John Doe."

Bob DuPont made sanitary silicone tubing systems and sold in 1995. Sales were $12+ million. The buyer was a public company with related businesses.

> One reason I sold is I don't want to be 80 years old by the time I get to the top of the mountain–I took it half-way up, and I wanted to bring in capital.
>
> Probably 95% of competitors that would be interested in your company will come in to learn about your business and not do a deal. You need a company in your industry that has some synergy–for example, they make nuts and you may make bolts. You don't want to bring a competi-

tor in and teach him anything because you will wind up paying a price—he will learn from you, and it will be a cheap marketing study, and then he'll walk away from a deal.

I don't want to be 80 years old when I get to the top of the mountain . . .

Selling a small business is very treacherous—it could destroy your company if you ever had to take it back. I think the most important thing is to make sure you don't have to take it back.

Once the price is set you should let the accountants and the lawyers handle all the details, and when they run into a hiatus, then they can come to you. Never have a confrontation. Listen to their side of it, as they are going to listen to yours. Remember, they are buying something and they only know how you are doing from what is on paper. And they don't know who is going to stay, and who is not going to stay.

What you want to do is protect the people who made you, and that is a major consideration.

□

Richard Dempster made products that clean air; he sold in 1992. Sales were about $40 million. The purchaser was a corporation with sales in the billions.

I had one very hot business. I had three businesses, and one of them, which I started in 1986, grew very fast. It had an 85% compounded growth rate per annum, and it was earning about 20% after tax. So it was a very attractive business, with very strong cash flows.

. . . at the outset, you are selling, not negotiating . . .

Once your company is known to be in play and that you are interested in selling, the phone rings and the mail piles up because there are a jillion people out there anxious to play a role. They generally fall into three categories: one, there seem to be a lot of independent guys with a secretary and a mailbox who purport to be in the business; secondly, there are firms like Geneva, for example, who work very hard at selling small and mid-sized companies; and then there are the Ivy-League sorts of firms, generally investment banking firms, who all are very interested in selling businesses, although if your business is too small they tend to walk away from it–they don't want to spend the time on anything that isn't a pretty considerable size.

I found that you learn a lot if you ask all of those whom you contact–or those who contact you–for referral lists, people whose businesses they have sold. I called a couple of dozen individuals who had sold businesses through various intermediaries. That was my research.

I felt that the businesses were worth a lot more money than some people were telling me they were worth.

I was only going to sell these businesses once. The research was worth doing. I felt that the businesses were worth a lot more money than some people were telling me they were worth. It turns out I was right. I must say that from my experience the investment banking firms don't work quite as hard as some of the smaller organizations that make all their living selling businesses. They seem to dig harder, they sell harder, and they spend an inordinate amount of time working at it, whereas the investment banking firms do a general mailing, and bla bla . . . I don't think they work as hard.

If you have a business worth up to $90 million, then you really need someone that is going to work very hard at selling your business. I would tend to stay away from the major investment banking firms, and go with someone smaller–I have a bias at the moment toward the Geneva Company. They don't have the same classy label, but they sure do work hard at selling your business.

You have got to get past the people who just crunch numbers . . .

I think also that the entrepreneur–or whoever has the upfront style in the selling company–is going to do most of the selling anyway. You have to put yourself in front of a lot of people, you've got to be enthusiastic, and you really have to generate enthusiasm, and sell your company.

The ideal companies, the ones I thought should buy my company and put the highest value on it, were not interested when first contacted by mail or telephone. Partially that is because you wind up talking to mergers and acquisitions, or financial, people. It is very difficult to get through to the operating people—who would understand how their business and yours could make music.

One of the secrets is that you have got to get past the people who just crunch numbers and get to the people who understand the market, the products, and the business.

I have many, many years of experience in industry associations, boards of directors, and I know lots of people in the operating ranks of *Fortune* 500 companies. You need someone who can go to the board of directors or the chief executive and say, "This really makes sense. Listen to me." And get a good hearing. I found that the companies that I thought should be interested were just crossing it off, for a variety of reasons. And I made it a point to go to some of these companies that had brushed it off and get through to some operating executives. I talked to them, showed them what it was all about, and, lo and behold, I had them going upstairs to the M&A or financial people, and saying, "We really ought to take a look at this because this really makes sense, and I think it is a downstream winner."

I did the selling in the end.

So I wound up paying a lot of money to people for marketing my company, and I did the marketing in the end. I did the selling in the end. You can't sit back and expect someone else to do a good job. They may or may not hit a home run. But I would say that they are going to get a two-base hit, and if you want to hit a home run you better get out there and take a few cuts at it yourself.

You want to be sure you get the maximum value before it peaks.

The timing of the sale was influenced by my own age—and the company was red hot. You want to be sure you get the maximum value before it peaks. Not that my company was imminently going to peak, but I just thought that it was a good time all around.

There were a lot of people who began to recognize how well we were doing, and that attracts competition. Potential entrants were everywhere in the world and they were very, very big. They could deploy resources in the business that would really dwarf mine, and so it would be important to tuck my company into a big one that had substantial resources, and could seize the opportunity to globalize the business more quickly than I would have been able to do.

The negotiations took a long time because I would sit with one lawyer and across the table would be ten lawyers and two financial types. They spent a lot of time looking at the hole in the doughnut, instead of looking at the doughnut.

Top issues for a seller are, one, presentation. Put it together in the most marketable and sensible package. You have to have a package that represents what you are selling. I think how you present that is very, very important.

> . . . you have to describe it as you would if you were selling a product . . .

A book was prepared–and paid for–for me, and I threw it out and did it myself. You have to market your business, you have to describe it as you would if you were selling a product. The package I paid for was boring as hell, missed all the romance, and just got into a lot of statistical data that buried the real opportunity. At the outset, you are selling, not negotiating. The first thing you have to do is get some attention.

Secondly, who you get to help you do the selling is critical. And if you are selling for less than $90 million, I would get someone who really hustles companies, and works hard at it. I would not get the second team in a major investment banking firm–they are going to be interested in frying bigger fish.

> . . . all you're really asking someone else to do is help you get in front of the right buyers.

The third thing I would concentrate on is the recognition that in the final analysis you really have to do most of it yourself. You're really the spokesman, and all you're really asking someone else to do is help you get in front of the right buyers.

□

Bob Yarnall made valves and sold in 1986 for about $100 million to a publicly owned company with related businesses.

Find the optimum partner who will treat your old colleagues well.

Drive a hard bargain. Be willing to pay capital gains taxes.

As the ancient black pitcher Satchel Paige said, "Don't never look back–sumthin' might be gainin' on yu."

□

Michael Mintz and his brother made medical devices (sales: $15+ million) and sold in 1991. The buyer was a public company with sales of more than $1 billion.

Plan to sell your business from the very outset because your attitude in building a business is different from a plan to keep the business for the family.

The primary thing is to make yourself fungible. You have to be sure that when a new owner takes over the business it is not wholly dependent on your expertise.

I hired Gerry Feldman with the idea that he, number one, could prepare the business, in an appropriate way, to be attractive, and, number two, could represent a part of permanent management that was not an owner or founder. Owners and founders, in general, are probably not suitable employees in an acquired company. My brother and I were not there two years after the closing.

. . . make yourself fungible . . .

We had a very good investment banker who prepared the "book" that described the company, and made it attractive to an acquirer. I think this was essential. Investment bankers know what acquirers' attitudes are, and what they are looking for.

Why are you selling if this is such a good deal?

The buyer is always asking himself what is there about this used car that he is not telling me. There is always the question, "Why are you selling this if this is such a good deal?" Handling the answer to this question is very delicate. Sometimes it is very apparent. In our case, I saw at that stage that it had reached a sales volume and value which would provide my brother and me with all of the funds which we would need for the rest of our lives. And this is what I told the buyer. He took this with a grain of salt–but the investment banker was useful here too as he could divert the conversation away from this issue.

When you have built a business over 20 years, it is hard to convince a buyer that your ego is not tied up in it.

At the outset I wanted to sell by age 55. We were a year late. We had to address an appropriate window of opportunity–we had to have the growth curve to attract the buyer, and we had to have the ability to recognize the window of opportunity. The new manager's assignment was to prepare the business for sale–with a five-year contract.

. . . buyers can take advantage of a neophyte . . .

In the negotiations–the dances and the games that buyers will play, especially skillful buyers such as the one who bought our company, who have acquired many companies, and know the footwork of the dance–buyers can take advantage of a neophyte who in his lifetime may sell one or two companies.

The buyer is going to be looking for these little chinks in your armor.

Anything that appears to be a weakness will be an issue. There was, for example, an undisclosed contract–not intentionally undisclosed–which we had failed to disclose in the book. It was not, in our opinion, a big issue; however, it was an issue that was used by the buyer to lower the price. We at that point had to go into our side of the dance and say, "If it means that much to you, maybe it means that much to us, and perhaps we shouldn't sell it to you." It ended up costing me a lot.

It is important to be very objective in going through your books, and having advice from the investment banker. Some things are going to escape you, but they are not going to escape the buyer. The buyer is going to be looking for these little chinks in your armor.

The cost of these services was returned to us many times over.

I cannot stress enough the importance of securing competent legal counsel. Preparation of the final sales document is every bit a part of the negotiations. We interviewed five law firms before settling on Jacobson & Mermelstein in Manhattan. These experienced professionals caught every nuance in the sales documents, and negotiated a generous catch-all "basket" for our representations and warranties. The cost of these services was returned to us many times over.

□

A. J. Lane made sophisticated switchgear and sold in the mid-1980's to a successful, demanding, publicly-owned manufacturing company. Sales were about $14 million. Eight years later, he was still running the business for the new owner.

In selling a business, you have to deal first with the emotions–what it is you want to do as a person, as the owner. After working for yourself, it is difficult to decide to go back and work for someone else. You have to get past that hurdle. Then once you start looking for the best buyer, one of the problems is you get too many people wanting to help you sell your business.

In my case, a company that I liked came to me. We had a good mutual business fit. Strategically, they had some things that I really needed: in particular, a national sales force (mine was more regional), and they had some products that were very complementary to the product line that we were selling. I could see that the combination could make a much better business. And the other people were really eager to have me join them, which made the negotiations much more friendly than if it were one-sided. It was a two-sided proposition, which is the ultimate best way to do something like this.

I have my cake, and I could eat it, too.

For the price, I brought in a couple of people who were merger and acquisition specialists. One I knew personally–and he had a friend in the business, and I consulted him, too. So I got a couple of outside opinions about what the business was worth. Also, I had just bought the business a year and a half earlier, and I had some idea of the right price. The parent company that sold me the business thoroughly researched the market, as they wanted it to be an arms-length transaction because I was an employee. They brought in a study team, and did a fairly extensive review.

So, in this case, within a year and a half, I had a professional study, and a couple of outside opinions. This gave a range of price that was reasonable. Ultimately, it became a reasonable price for both of us.

. . . get away from the business, with a third party, to price it . . .

It is important, I think, that you get away from the business, with a third party, to price it. When you own something, you always think it is worth a lot more than outsiders think it is worth. You have to get the emotion out, get the numbers, and consider the long-term prospects—and look yourself really honestly in the mirror and see the warts and pimples, and the things that aren't really so great about your company.

For me it was a great experience, because I could do this, put the "retirement account" in the bank, and go on and work for someone with a free mind.

The company had been unprofitable for about eight years prior to my buying it, and from the first quarter I bought the company, it turned around, and continued to make accelerating profits. This was doing what is being done widely today—trimming overheads, taking unnecessary operations out, concentrating on the businesses we did best, instead of a wide variety of things they were trying to do. When I bought the company we cleaned up a lot of old inventory, and old debts, and other things hanging over eight years of unprofitable operations.

Starting with a clean blackboard, and making immediate cuts in fringe benefits, and numbers of people, and things like that, gave us an immediate profit focus, and by the time some of these other ideas cut in, we stopped doing some of the garbage jobs, we got a new computer, and put in some intelligent programs to see what our costs really were. A combination of those things put management in control.

I don't know if a seller could take these steps to prepare his business for sale. Before I bought the company, I was a group vice-president, and this was one of my divisions. I had brought in three general managers over a five-year period, and I couldn't get a turn-around, and I couldn't get anyone to listen to my ideas. I did the next best thing. I bought it and did it myself.

. . . you have to decide what is going to satisfy you in life . . .

I think you have to decide what is going to satisfy you in life. For a lot of people, they have to get to their mid-forties to decide what they want to be when they grow up. Once you decide that, and you can live with yourself–and not have to be the super CEO of some company, or some other goal. It was a career change to buy the business, and another one when I sold it–going back to work for someone else. You have to soul-search that a little bit, and make sure that you, your wife and the family are going to be happy with being put back into this position.

For me it was fine. I considered the situation, took an employment contract for three years, continued to run the company, and still do eight years later. It has worked out: I have my cake, and I could eat it, too.

. . . do you hang on and try and make a killing?

Over the years the most common question I have had is, "Are you satisfied? Are you happy now that you don't own the company?" And I have to say I have no regrets. People say I could have gotten more, "Look how much the company has grown." I point out to them that at the time I sold there were some dark clouds on the horizon, also. It may not have been as good as this eight years later. You never know: it is like selling a stock, do you sell after you have made a few points, or do you hang on and try and make a killing?

□

Alexander Ariniello made equipment to pressurize telephone cables and sold in 1988 to a public company. Sales were about $6 million.

I would advise going to one of these seminars put on by companies like Geneva. I went to one and learned a lot. I didn't sell the business through them–but the seminar was very helpful in how to price the business, how to negotiate, and so forth.

The buyer found us. One of these merger and acquisition brokers contacted us by letter, and he was paid by the buyer.

I would advise going to one of these seminars put on by companies like Geneva . . .

Looking back I would not have done anything differently. It worked out well. We had three principals, and we each had three-year employment contracts. The only problem we had was there was a change in the chief executive in the company that bought our business. That changed things. The chief executive at the time of our deal wanted to build up their telecommunications business. The new chief executive de-emphasized that side of the business. They moved it from Colorado to California and ruined it. It was later sold.

. . . sell it to grow it . . .

Top issues for a seller are pricing the business, working with the new owners, and being realistic–about the future of the business, and whether you should sell it, and perhaps sell it to grow it. Sometimes you don't have the internal resources to grow the business.

□

John Henning made training and simulation equipment and sold to a public company in 1994. Sales were about $10 million.

First of all, know what it is you are going after, believe in it totally–and have patience. I had specific concerns for protection of key personnel that were here as members of the family of this organization, and obviously I had concerns to assure myself of equitable consideration for my future so that I would have no problems financially.

. . . it was probably 2½ to 3 years before the sale was made . . .

It can take considerable time from first getting acquainted with the acquirer, and them getting acquainted with your business, and then understanding each other, and who you are truly dealing with. For us it took around 18 months. You probably are talking of 6 months to a year, at least–and unexpected things come up, with respect to cash flow of the buyer. They are not going to expose all of that to you, but you have to be prepared for such issues to impact the timing. When I made my decision to sell, it was probably around 2½ to 3 years before the sale was made.

Top three issues for a seller: know what it is you need for yourself; know what things you want for the business; and know who you want to sell to–a company that is interested in developing the company, or a company only interested in certain pieces of it, with the rest dumped on the side.

□

Richard McClellan was a principal in a computer terminal company with $90 million in sales; this business was sold in 1978 to a large public company. In the mid 1980's he was president (and principal) of a company with sales of about $15 million that made motion-control products; it was sold in 1986 to a public company with sales of more than $1 billion.

As an independent businessman, you have a certain psychological mindset that you develop towards running a business. With a new owner, no matter how supportive, or hands-off, the new people are, there is somebody looking over your shoulder, and it ain't going to be the same. I was running a business for a new owner, and wanted a new $2,000 desktop computer. All computer purchases had to be approved at headquarters half-way across the country. The business I was running had $50 million in sales, and the decisions made, or not made, without consulting headquarters made $2,000 seem paltry, but the mindset of the organization required approvals for prescribed actions.

. . . there are probably six months when the chief executive and the chief financial officer spend 20% of their clock time on the process, but the mental energy is damn near 100%.

I think the better deals come about when the seller is approached as a result of a buyer's search, as opposed to retaining someone and putting up a for-sale sign.

Even in the best of circumstances–and they don't all happen; it ain't over 'til it's over–there are probably six months when the chief executive and the chief financial officer spend 20% of their clock time on the process, but the mental energy is damn near 100%.

. . . it ain't going to be the same . . .

I have always been in technology companies, and I think that if you are going to get acquired, it is really far better to be acquired by someone who is acquiring you for your technology as opposed to someone who is making a financial acquisition.

First and foremost of the top issues is, "Can you live with the folks? Do they seem to do business in the same way you do?" I think that is extraordinarily important.

> . . . the success rate of independent CEO's who become happy and successful as division managers ain't very good.

I would say a responsible seller would make certain that someone working in the business can run it. He ought to operate it with the assumption that he, the owner, is going to leave. Therefore he needs management continuity for ethical and financial reasons. If you look at the success rate of independent CEO's who become happy and successful as division managers, it ain't very good. You ought to have one person–preferably two–who could run the business. The last company I sold–it had sales of about $16 million at the time–had two people able to run it, and both were in turn promoted to division manager.

> . . . you want them to value you . . .

You probably have to walk away from negotiations once. I think it is important that you get a good price–because you are going to be the property of some larger company, you want them to value you.

All deals take place when each side thinks they are getting more than they are giving. There may be a range where both sides believe that, but you have to get in that range. And close to the middle of it is what you want.

□

Robert Girvin made mountain bikes (sales about $8 million) and sold in 1993 to a public company with sales of about $500 million.

Make sure you have a business that is salable–and that is not always the case. People often want to bail out when things have become so bleak that they are overbearing. This is not the time to sell. The time to sell is when things look great and promising, there is a good story to tell, and your back is not up against the wall and you have to sell because your bank is about to pull your loan.

I should have talked to more buyers.

If you really intend to sell, the best way is to plan ahead and position your company so that it is attractive to someone who will step up and pay you some real money for it.

We were undercapitalized. We were very much positioned in a niche–bikes with suspension systems–that was about to take off. I thought we had the opportunity to take that from $8 million in sales to $50 million in sales over 3 to 5 years, but to finance that via my local banker just did not compute. No way you were going to do it. The business requires a lot of capital, especially to finance imported parts with long lead times. There appeared to be no option. I had cultivated a niche in the market, and there was a very good story to be told.

The biggest changes in my working life are not having to worry about debt, and having a lot of capital available. This changed my comfort level more than anything else.

I should have talked to more buyers. I think my problem was fear of having my customers and my competitors hear that we were for sale, and that that could have had a negative spin on our position in the market. And so I was overly protective of that knowledge and afraid to let that out. In hindsight, I would probably have done better to have gotten the word out into the market, and I think I could have ended up with a couple of other major players bidding for the business, and that could have made a big difference in the ultimate price.

I had a good friend in the merger and acquisition game advising me on the sidelines, and that was exactly his advice. I was just afraid to take it. He was right, and I regret that I did not listen to him more carefully. I didn't believe him that it was in my best interest to let it be more widely known that the company was for sale.

The top three issues for a seller are (1) Make sure that you are negotiating with someone who truly has the financial horsepower to do the deal; (2) Get as much money as you can up front–a bird in the hand is worth two in the bush; and (3) If you are going to continue to be involved, make sure that you are comfortable with the people. I'd put them in that order.

□

George Nichols sold a maker of plastic parts in 1986. Sales were about $32 million. The buyer was a public company.

The first advice I would give is to make sure you *want to* sell the business. That is a chapter all by itself. A very personal decision. Some people retire, and then are lost about what to do with their life. This is a time to get as much advice as you possibly can: professional advice, not advice from friends.

You ought to get legal advice about how it should be structured. Accountants advise on the taxes. And you need investment advice about how to invest the money. Is the buyer going to want assistance?

You want the new company to be successful. You want your employees left in the company to be successful. You want to take that into account in your planning.

My God! I set the price too low . . .

The timing was picked for me. About half of our sales were to the automotive industry. The industry was at that time down-sizing the number of their vendors, and they wanted each vendor to take more responsibility: to get involved in products at an earlier stage–engineering the products, etc. In order to do that successfully we would have had to grow the company, and we were not able to grow it internally, so I was out looking for other businesses to acquire.

There are relatively few companies interested in buying a particular business . . .

At the same time, the principals of a competitor happened to call me. The president of the company that owned the competitor called and asked if they could talk about acquiring my business. I said "No, the business is not for sale. I need to grow, too." We talked for about 45 minutes about the changes in the industry, and how we had both come to the same conclusion about the need to be larger. We ended the conversation with me asking to buy his subsidiary.

Meanwhile I had a handshake-deal on another company to buy. They had reached the limit of their ability to grow. I had $4 million of business that I could put in their plant. They changed their mind and wanted to wait a year to sell. That collapsed.

Friday of that week I met Ernst & Whinney. They said this is a sellers' market. Monday morning I called the company I had been talking to. I said, "I might be like a nervous bride: you might get me into the bedroom, or even into the bed, and I might then shriek and fall out."

We got much more than an average price.

They were very honorable. No leaks–and that was very important to me. Our employees were nifty people. We employed 187 people.

We got much more than an average price. They paid more than that company was worth. We did a five-year forecast, and looked at what our earnings would be.

The negotiations were fun. They asked how much I wanted for the company. I said, "a lot." They asked what I would be happy with, and I asked for three or four days to come up with that number.

I got some advice. I called and told them I had determined a number–and I added some what-ifs. I had only two employees in their sixties, and I said they had to agree to employ them until they were 65, and I said there would be some other things similar to that.

They took the number, and called back that night, and said, "You've got a deal." I set the number, and it was a number I was thrilled with. They accepted the number the same day. I thought, "My God! I set the price too low." I thought for a day, and I called them back. This is one of the closest calls of my life: I almost blew the deal. I told them I had met with my accountant, and I thought one part of the deal was tax-free, and it turns out that it is not, and so I am going to need an additional $500,000 to pay the taxes. And I almost blew the deal. They said, "I don't think we can do that."

I said, "I do not want to sell unless I can get the amount I had in mind after taxes. If you can't do that, please wrap up my papers and send them back to me." He said, "Do you mean to say you would jeopardize the whole deal for $500,000?" And I said to him, "Do you mean you would jeopardize this whole deal for $500,000?"

When I hung up the phone I felt terrible.

The following day I got a call. They said I was making it very difficult for them. I said this was not my intent. I said my intent was to obtain a number, a target I had set–otherwise, I was going to continue to operate, and to continue to grow, and make profits. The Management Committee, on a split vote, agreed to one thing: "We believe you did this in good faith, but we do not believe you should let this deal go for $500,000." They offered $250,000 more. I said, "Let me think about that." They said, "Think about it!" I hung up the phone, and shouted for joy. They let me off the hook for the stupid thing I did. I waited a day. I called them back and accepted the deal.

I would not have done that if I had to do it all over again–it wasn't worth it for my health for those two days.

One man's garbage is another man's find.

I did not talk to any other buyers. A business is not a commodity, and not like a beautiful painting that a lot of people would appreciate and bid for in an auction. There are relatively few companies that are interested in buying a particular business.

I bought this company in 1980 from a billion-dollar company. It was a stepchild. One man's garbage is another man's find. About six years later I sold it to another billion-dollar company.

One of the things I am most proud of is that at the closing every employee got $100 for every month of service in the company. And the salaried people, who put in many extra hours, also got a bonus equal to 10% of their cumulative income on their W-2's since the time I bought the company. The general manager got $70,000, and the lowest level manager got $6,000. The after-tax cost of the entire bonus plan was about $400,000. I recognized the valuable contributions that others had made to the success of the company.

I sold assets, but I kept the receivables–and the payables. The buyer collected the receivables and paid the payables for me. This took about six months.

I planned to buy another business–I was 53 when I sold the company. But I lost the killer instinct. My wife died, and perhaps I faced my own mortality. If you are to succeed in business, you need to take every advantage that you can, legally and morally. But you must have the instinct, "I'm going to stomp on him . . . beat my competitor. . . . I am going to serve that customer. . . . I am not going to lose that customer for anything. . . ." You've got to be sure your vendors are not slipping one past you. You really need that killer instinct. I looked at some businesses, but it was not there.

My plan was to buy another company, but I have not done it. I had a plan, but the plan changed.

□

Jim Cullen was chief executive of a company in Ireland owned by institutions. This company sold several businesses, including, in 1994, a maker of molded cable assemblies with sales of about $13 million and plants in Connecticut and Ireland. The buyer was a publicly owned U.S. company.

I have eleven points:

1. Professional presentation is important. Documents should be clear and understandable. It should be a professional presentation.
2. You should show confidence in yourself and in your company. People like dealing with winners.
3. You should prepare the company and the management. Bring the people on stream, and get them to support the sale.
4. You cannot rush the situation. Whether you like it or not, it is going to take a year to 18 months. It is unusual if it is less.
5. Find out what the other guy wants. What is his agenda? What is he trying to achieve?

. . . you cannot rush the situation . . .

6. Avoid lawyers and accountants wherever possible until the last minute. Keep them away from everything, and try to get the commercial aspects of the deal done before you bring all these guys in.
7. Get to the guy who is making the decision.

8. A facilitator, like a broker, is very important. Someone who can listen to both sides. He can get the buyer's negative points, and positive points. The buyer might be more open in talks with the facilitator than in talks with the seller.
9. A broker can research the market. He can ask if a buyer would be interested in a type of company without revealing the name–something the principal cannot do.

. . . hit them back with the information as soon as possible.

10. Respond quickly. If a buyer visits, and then asks for certain data–hit them back with the information as fast as possible. It keeps the pressure on the buyer to move on to the next step.
11. Get the buyer to spend money as soon as possible–on research and things like that. The more money they spend, the better–for travel, legal expenses, etc.

□

Martin Gould sold a biotechnology company in 1994 to a small public company with related businesses. The company made proprietary tests to detect contaminants in food. Sales were about $1 million.

First thing you have to do, before you go out to sell your company, is to sit down and figure out what the strengths of your company are, and what the weaknesses are.

. . . find a buyer that fills those weaknesses . . .

Then you have to find a way to make the perception of your strengths stronger than they are, and you have to take the weaknesses and gloss over them, and make like they are easy things to fix. Find a buyer that fills those weaknesses. You have to be very honest with yourself, find that person, and constantly ingratiate yourself–stress how good they are in certain areas so that every time they bring up the weaknesses you say, "Yeah, but you're really good at that," and it gets whitewashed.

You are never sure when something is done.

Then when you do join, after the fact, it will work, which is important that you have a nice sale afterwards. Because things can always boomerang. America is litigious. You are never sure when something is done.

You have to have your accounting spotless. People usually don't. If they had the money to have a good accountant, to have everything perfect, they would go public, or they would put the money in products, or sales and marketing, and wouldn't be on the market to sell.

If you want to sell a company, you really ought to take time out and just bite the bullet and learn how to do the financials yourself so that you can present them and know the numbers. It's not that hard to learn. People who are good at other parts of the business can do it. If not, you have to come up with someone and share the task. If the numbers aren't right, buyers will walk away. My numbers in this business weren't done right, even though I had a CPA do them.

Have your technology, sales, and marketing in line–have control over these things. So that you can present it as a real business.

And find someone who can match the right parties. Someone who is a dealmaker.

There are people out there who are looking for good ideas, who want to take good ideas, not put two people together–but they present themselves as people looking to put people together, and really all they want to do is to find good ideas: either to take over that company, or watch the company die, and steal the ideas. And you have to be careful of those people, because they are swimming around in the pool.

Don't judge too soon.

And just talk, talk, talk–talk to everybody. Don't close the door on anybody. Don't think you are so smart that you can tell this guy is going to be a dead end, and this guy–because he drives a BMW–he's the good guy. And this guy over here drives a Lumina, and he's nobody. Don't judge too soon.

□

Jim Anthony made gauges and instruments (for boats and off-highway equipment) and sold to a public company in 1986. Sales were about $7 million.

The first thing to do is put everything in order. Depending on the size of the company, a seller should reach out to one of the bigger firms to review everything. Goldman Sachs or one of the other big investment companies might do that. I didn't do that, but I should have. I missed getting a much broader number of people interested in the business, and a more competitive picture. There were probably people who would have been interested in the business that I never contacted. I probably sold to the wrong company.

I have run into two or three people who used national firms, who paid $25,000-$50,000 for them to come and look the business over. Then they reached out to buyers all over the country, and they made much better deals than if they had just sold through a local person.

I missed getting a much broader number of people interested . . .

For example, if I had gone to a national outfit, I probably would have had OMC or Brunswick very interested in buying the company. It might have been a bidding contest. This is hindsight. I would have felt I got the best price for the business. But you also have to look at what they are going to do with the company.

The company that bought my business was taken over by an LBO group, and I am not happy about that. They probably overpaid for the company, and they took away a profit-sharing plan from the employees, and limited their capital for expansion.

I probably sold to the wrong company . . .

I could have sold the company for more money to a different buyer, but this company wanted to bring in their own people to replace my managers. I wanted my people to have the chance to build the business, and be independent. The buyer gave me the impression that they would leave them alone. They left them alone so much that they never came and audited anything when they bought it. I should have been suspicious right there.

I was very remiss about one thing, in hindsight. I was 62 when I sold. They paid me a consulting fee for three years. When I was with the company, I gave the top three or four executives a supplemental pension plan, to give them 50% of their salary at retirement. I did not take that myself because I figured I could stay with the company all my life and be taken care of. The pension that I have is minimal. I should have insisted on better pension arrangements, and I think they would have accepted it very readily.

The top issues for me were security for the company and the employees, and security for my own family.

□

"John Doe" sold a wholesaler of consumer products in 1987. Sales were some $75 million. The buyer was a public company.

Get your books in order–get all the skeletons out of the closet. Make sure it's clean. Then, take a walk to Wall Street. Just make the rounds for an experience that gives you an idea of what you can begin to ask for the business. Brush up on the numbers, make sure you have the right accountants, and the right advice, even before you choose a broker, to make sure you know what you can tell the broker.

Once the books are in order, and everything is clean and up to snuff, and you have at least a three-year performance record, then you can put the feelers out.

If you are too small to interest the Wall Street people they will tell you politely that they have too much on their plate at the present time. Glamour helps. Wholesale has no glamour. I was selling philosophy, management and growth.

> . . . I had a hook in the buyer, and I played him for over a year . . .

You have to be totally honest with potential buyers. You can't play games. You have got to let them do their due diligence. You know a deal can fall through because the buyer says you didn't tell us this, or you didn't tell us that.

It's basic common sense. The best advice is to read up on how to sell a business. There are publications that tell you what to look for.

I had a consultation with somebody from up north to put a price on the business. Not that I used it, but it was a starting point. It was an education process. Somebody who had sold a business and had a book that took you through certain steps. My statements were cleaned up, I had no long-term debt, the inventory was cleaned up, and everything else was running smoothly. It was like clockwork.

Then I went to Wall Street. I made all the rounds. I went to Oppenheimer, Bear Stearns, Drexel, and Lehman Brothers. And I really got an education. I was put to the task–questions, questions. . . . I mean it was a hell of an experience. The money people wanted me to stay with the business, give me a portion of the business to run it. I flatly refused. I only wanted to stay one year.

In negotiations you take a lot of gruff. They think you are a hayseed. A couple of guys from Wall Street flew in, and gave me the good-guy, bad-guy routine. I made a ball game out of it–they couldn't move me. You've got to stand your ground. They wanted all kinds of covenants restricting this and that.

I wanted my money up front. I just wanted to sell assets and the name. I still have the corporation today as a holding company. There are big-time tax advantages–you get the dividend exclusion, and other benefits. I have made a million dollars so far this year buying and selling stocks.

Guts, guts, guts . . . those are the top three issues for a seller. You've got to have guts to go in and face the music. You can't be browbeaten by Wall Street. They take you for a fancy lunch at Twenty-One, and you can be overpowered.

I really sold the business to his creditors.

I felt I had a hook in the buyer, and I played him for over a year. I really sold the business to his creditors.

□

Mayer Mitchell and associates sold a home-building business in 1972 to a public company with sales over $2 billion. The business had sales of more than $20 million. Five years later, he and his brother bought it back—and sold it again eight years later.

> If you are dealing with a major company, and they have you outgunned in their knowledge of acquisitions, go get yourself the best expert in that particular field to represent you because you will do it one time, and they have probably done it many times. That is what I did with Ken Leventhal.
>
> Ken Leventhal represented me when I decided I was going to do something—either go public, sell, or merge. I hired him to come down and get my books into a modality of a public company. He was an expert in real estate, so, we being in real estate development, that is why we went to him.
>
> We sold for stock the first time in 1972, and it had some unforeseen consequences when the stock price collapsed a year or two later, but we took the advice of our advisor and we sold 25% of the stock we received within a week of the merger.
>
> . . . and hope it is the worst sale they ever make . . .
>
> That was Ken Leventhal's advice. That was our book value, and then we could ride on the house. If anyone merged with a company in exchange for stock, I would recommend that they secure the same right: do it, sell, and hope it is the worst sale they ever make—because they will be riding with 75% of the acquisition price in stock. But if it goes down, then they haven't been blasted.
>
> We sold in June of 1972—we had a five-year employment contract—and we bought it back in January of 1977. We had made a commitment to fulfill the five-year employment contract, and we did.
>
> We bought it back because the buyer's stock price had collapsed, and they needed to get out of the real estate business, and we had no intention of staying with the company.
>
> So we did an LBO, and they provided us, through a joint venture, with a significant amount of capital, which gave us a base, and a company that was already in operation, and we paid a premium for that.

The seller financed 95% of the price. We had 100% of their assets under our management when we were working for them; they thought that if they financed 95% of the assets, and we were working for ourselves, that they would not have a problem getting their money back. It worked out well, and we paid them off early.

We were going to take cash, or not sell . . .

We sold again in 1985–for cash. We had the experience of the first deal, and we said we simply were not going to take stock, or any subordinated debentures, or anything. We were going to take cash, or not sell. That was in effect the last round-up, and we were not going to subject ourselves to the vagaries of the market.

The top three issues for a seller are the price, residual liabilities, and a long-term employment contract. Those were the three most important elements to me. In our case, the price was the third element. Our position was, "No long-term employment contract, no residual liabilities, all cash," and then, "How much?"

□

Art Bollinger was a partner in a maker of ultrasound medical diagnostic devices with sales of $12+ million. It was sold in 1990 to a public company with related interests.

Selling a business is a complicated process–it is not cut-and-dried. To find a broker or someone to market your business takes a lot of time to set up. They are not in the yellow pages. That process needs to be done thoroughly and carefully to find a relationship that you are comfortable with.

If you own a business you get a lot of calls from people off-the-cuff, and you get a feel for the availability of people. I think there is a marketing process that goes on in the business of brokers. And they market their skills, they make phone calls. We were approached by several people. The way they approached us gave us some impressions about the way they did business.

We wanted to stay with the business, and continue to see it grow and prosper, and we sold to a company that we felt could continue that process. They had marketing resources in our particular line. I thought their marketing outlets could help us, and continue the product growth. We were having trouble making that next big step into a larger business, and we were thinking and hoping that the association would help us make that jump.

. . . they wanted us to continue to work like it was ours . . .

Going back to work for somebody else was different and a little difficult. We didn't understand how their head was screwed on, and their requirements for the future. The corporate environment was not what we thought it was before we sold. We thought that we would be getting assistance and help, and instructions and guidance, but we did not. We were just stuck out there all alone. But we couldn't make the decisions that we previously had made. It was no longer our business–it was their business, yet they wanted us to continue to work like it was ours. It was a hard transition to make. We fought like crazy, within the framework they set up for this, to try and make a profitable business out of it. They didn't particularly understand what we were trying to do, and how we were trying to do it, but they didn't mind butting in and trying to design our interests.

I would try to negotiate a price up front with the lawyers.

I would try to negotiate a price up front with the lawyers. If you leave it open, the pricing is based not on the hours spent but on the perceived value to the seller. When you go to the broker you know pretty much what it is going to cost you, but when you go into the legal system–unless it is negotiated up front–the price can vary pretty widely.

Company compatibility has to be the first major issue for a seller. Nobody wants to see a company fail, or change significantly, after it is sold. You want to try and maintain that relationship with the employees. Two has to be financial considerations. Everyone has to be happy with the purchase price. We talked about percentages of profit, or multiples of profit, profit over five years, but nobody really knows what it is. It really comes down to the amount of money the purchaser can borrow, based on the cash flow, to pay off the acquisition.

Compatibility–you cannot say enough about it. You have to be compatible with the people who acquire the business. Sometimes you would take less money to make sure the association was strong for the future. You want to be sure that the people who buy your business are very much aware of what you are doing, how you are doing it, and that the information is there from the past for them to evaluate. That does indicate that there is some preparation involved. You can't just go out and sell it. You have to have some preparation–that includes audited books, a history of profitability, and a history of growth.

□

Ken West sold a custom blender of minerals in 1992. Sales were $18 million. The buyer was a larger public company with related interests.

We were a family business with 35 employees. I was in partnership with my son. I was 65 and wanted to retire. I gave my son the option of running the business, or selling it. He was a full partner. It looked like we had to spend a lot of money for new equipment, technical help, etc. We decided to sell.

We got 71% up front, and the rest was an eight-year earn-out.

At first we talked to a competitor, a very big company. We screwed around with them for about a year, and they dropped us–but it was out on the street that we were for sale. Everyone wanted to buy us because they knew we had an interesting chunk of the market–even a Japanese company came to us.

Then we talked to another company for about a year–and that fell through. And then they came back to us, and our profits had gone up–I said, "The price of poker has just gone up." As a result we got another $4 million out of it. We were happier than hell.

Sales are now off 30%, and my son is under some pressure from the new owners. His life has changed a lot–marketing meetings, planning meetings, lots of traveling–and lots of things we didn't do as a small family business.

. . . I think the attorneys did blow the first deal . . .

In the first negotiations, a tough old son-of-a-bitch tried to beat us into the ground. Both lawyers were hard-nosed, trying to get the better of each other, and didn't want to give in. He was of course trying to protect our interests, but I criticized my lawyer. I think the attorneys did blow the first deal–no one would give in. Use your own good discretion in dealing with lawyers. Have the lawyers keep you from getting into legal problems. Most lawyers are on somewhat of an ego trip. They get into these things, and they think it is like a big game–and they want to win. They want ups on everybody. I wanted to get rid of the business. I used to get on the phone to my attorney and say, "Phil, don't blow this thing. I want out, and I want out now. I am willing to give in on that point and this point." He had a hard time giving in.

The first buyer kept flipping things in and out of the contract. The last one they gave me required me to work six months out of the year, and I was not interested in that. We rewrote the contract to our liking, and they said they were not interested in going ahead. A year later they came back and wanted to buy us–at our price. We said it was too late.

□

"John Doe" sold an environmental services business in 1982 for about $140 million to a larger public company in a related business.

We sold stock to raise capital, and developed the business into a $50-million company over ten or eleven years. The buyer went out and bought our stock. They got big by buying other companies. They bought many companies. Usually, when these people come in they have enough stock to have a good say in the deal.

> . . . you should be at 60% of your goal, at least, before you sell . . .

The worst time to sell a company is when you are just getting going. You would not get me to bite on that. The best time to get a good price for your business is when you have reached about 60% of your goals, in a profit mode. It is like crawling a ladder: you never want to sell it when you are first starting on the ladder because then you are just going to trade dollars. You want to get as near the top as you can before you sell a business, then you get your multiple.

> . . . you gotta leave something for the next guy.

You gotta leave something for the next guy. You should be at 60% of your goal, at least, before you sell. Sometimes you do not know what your top goal really is in a business. Sometimes it expands as time goes on.

□

Howard Slater sold an institutional pharmacy to a public company in 1994. Sales were about $5 million.

The time to sell is when business is going well–it should be on an upswing. If it is not on an upswing, you are not going to get your money out of it. People are only interested in buying businesses that are good and growing.

> . . . the most important advice was, "Make it a cash deal."

I think it is advantageous to have more than one or two buyers interested–not necessarily competing with each other. In our situation, we could have gotten more money from one of the companies interested in us, but we didn't feel it was a good marriage.

If you want to maintain the integrity of the business you have to pick the right buyer.

I did what most other people would do–I spoke to people who had been through the same thing. I got advice from them. I hired a well known local tax lawyer, and we used a law firm specializing in mergers and acquisitions as a consultant. The most important advice they gave me was "make it a cash deal. Don't take paper and don't take stock–when you have an opportunity to make a cash deal, do it."

□

Edward Yohman made power-conditioning equipment and sold in 1995 to a public company. Sales were $17+ million. A month after the closing, the buyer was itself acquired.

If you hire someone to sell your business, they don't care what they sell it for. It is make-a-buck-fast, as fast as you can, and turn it over. When you go to an agent or broker to sell your business you have got to recognize that his interest is not necessarily exactly the same as yours—he wants to get the job done, and do it fast. That's what I see.

> You should not allow the broker to state a price without your approval.

The second factor is the buyer has bought a number of businesses and knows the ins and outs and how to play the game. You, the seller, have not had a chance to think of all the factors involved—for example, here we set our sights too low, and we never put into the agreement the what-ifs that would normally be there. For example, "What if the buyer is itself acquired?" One month after we sold, the buyer was itself acquired by a much larger public company. What happens now to employment contracts, escrow accounts? The other guy, the buyer, has much more experience about the tax issues.

Another thing, the broker should not get a commission on the excess cash in the company—something we did not think about in advance.

If you have a bonus program for your employees, you have to ensure that it continues for a year at least to protect your employees.

You learn a lot, in hindsight. For example, if you have life insurance polices on key employees, it might be a good idea to transfer ownership of the policies out of the company, even though the premiums might no longer be tax-deductible. That is a lot better than sitting there and having the other guy own the policy—even if you leave the company, he can keep the policy.

The buyer asked our broker what he thought it would go for, and he gave a price. I had to negotiate up close to $6 million. You should not allow the broker to state a price without your approval.

> I found out that we set our sights too low.

Don't let them give you an asset deal. If you let them buy assets you pay more in taxes. The buyer of course prefers to buy assets so they can write up the assets for tax purposes.

I found out that we set our sights too low. I could have gotten a hell of a lot more. One of the factors involved was that I did not want to move this company. One company was offering us much more, but they wanted to move us within three years. I did not want that, so we went with this company to protect my employees.

We interviewed various brokers, and we found every one of them–one of the big accounting firms, one of the banks–was interested in selling the company as fast as they could. You have to be extremely careful in selecting your broker, checking out what they have done, and you set the price.

> He wants a win-win where he wins a little more than you do.

The buyer is cagey as hell, and that is normal. I have bought a couple of companies for our business. You are not going to be out there agreeing to everything the seller wants. The buyer is trying to get the best deal he can. But the buyer actually wants a win-win, if he is going to keep the people. He wants a win-win where he wins a little more than you do. If he has a win-lose, then he has just bought bricks and mortar, and that ain't going to work for him. The buyer really is going to try and get the best deal he can and make you think you got what you really wanted out of him. Afterwards, you know that when you really think about it, you could have negotiated a better deal. But that's all Monday-morning-quarterbacking.

They gave each of us three-year contracts, primarily for noncompete purposes.

We liked the buyer of our company because we would have been the top dog in their organization. We were going to be autonomous. Then, a month after our closing, they were acquired by a much larger public company, now, all of a sudden, we are in a quandary, we don't know what the hell is going on. We are getting memos all over the place, do this, do that. This new parent is an entirely different corporation than the company we sold to. They like to buy companies that make widgets, and they are excellent at squeezing them down to produce excellent cash flow. They automate companies to improve performance. But we are not a widget company. Our product is sophisticated and we often customize to meet requirements. Widget companies don't change anything.

They asked us to put 5% of the price in escrow for 18 months, in case there were EPA or other problems. We should have had an agreement that said if their company was acquired the escrow agreement was terminated.

What you ought to do is have an agreement with the broker that provides for a lower fee if you find the buyer on your own. I would not sign an exclusive arrangement with a broker again.

I wanted three things. I was looking at my future financial position. I wanted to maximize my financial return. Secondly, I didn't make this company, my employees made it for me, and so I had to look out for the employees and their future. Thirdly, I wanted a win-win—I think that it is very important. Otherwise, you can get acrimony.

□

Larry Cohoon was president and a principal of a company with a proprietary test for water quality. The business, with sales of around $5 million, was sold to a public company in 1993.

I think you need, first of all, a successful business, something that is salable.

We weren't necessarily trying to sell the business. We went out with an Offering Memorandum: we were looking for a strategic investor. The business had grown quite well in the U.S.: we were very profitable, and we were looking for international distribution rather than trying to set that up ourselves.

> . . . any company with the necessary wherewithal wanted to have control . . .

The business was throwing off quite a bit of cash. But the human resources were more of an issue than the cash to set up international distribution—and I wanted to go direct rather than through distributors. Also, we needed to add to our product line: through internal development, or getting technology or products outside. We were looking for a partner that could be helpful in R&D, and also acquiring or licensing other technologies, to put more in our basket to sell.

So, that is really what we started looking for. We were looking for an investment, but also a partner. As time went on, it became obvious that any company wanting to do that wanted to have control—and we were looking for a 20% equity position. Any company with the necessary wherewithal wanted to acquire control.

I won't say that sale was not in the back of our minds. I had two outside venture capital investors. The company had gone from bankruptcy to a fairly valuable business. It was profitable, and it was growing at better than 50% a year, and we knew that it was marketable. We did want to get a feel for what the market would pay for the company.

Is it adding value?

We used an investment banker to help us, and I think that is very helpful. If you have two CEO's, plus in my case venture capital investors, it is helpful if you have got someone who represents the company in the sale, or raising capital, because you can separate the personalities to get the initial negotiations moving forward. But I will say that in the end we all had to sit down at the table and make the final deal. I think it is better to have a third party represent you–at least in my experience.

One question to address is, "Is it adding value to the company that you sell? In the longer term, will it be more successful?" We exchanged our stock for theirs, so the sellers maintain an interest in the company. The question to ask is, "Is it going to be a stronger, larger, more profitable business down the road?"

A top issue is liquidity. We did it with a public company so we got publicly traded stock.

Another top issue is finding people you can work with, where the personalities fit. Because it is a "people-type" of transaction.

I did not want to run a division . . .

I enjoy running businesses. I did not want to run a division of a business. I had worked for a larger company before. I told the buyer I would stay on for the transition, but I did not want to stay on. If they had wanted five years, I would not have done the deal.

□

Jack Morris sold a producer of carpet cushion in 1986–sales were $60+ million. The buyer was a public company with related businesses.

If you are selling for stock, I think one of the absolute most important things is that you find a good management team–of the company that is buying you. This is the outstanding feature of the company that bought my company. The management is absolutely top-notch, and very honest–they are not trying to swindle anybody. They are open and above-board. Of course, if the selling party is selling to a public company and it is a substantial amount, then they should request a seat on their board of directors. They offered it to me, and I do sit on their board of directors. It was their thought to have me on the board.

> I wanted cash, but now I am happy I did not sell for cash.

It is preferable if the management team owns a substantial amount of the corporation that is buying your business. They have a greater interest in being aggressive with their company, and pushing it forward, when a lot of the stock is in management's hands. The company I sold to has 22-25% of their stock held by inside management. So it gives them a greater incentive to work harder and longer.

The buying company had progressed steadily, and their stock had increased gradually–and that is what someone selling a business for stock would want to look for.

> It is preferable if the management team owns a substantial amount of the corporation that is buying your business.

If you are selling to a public company, first check the management–be sure that the track record of the management and the company is good. And that they are people you can work with–they can understand your problems, and you can understand theirs.

I called them and asked if they would be interested in purchasing our company. And, of course, they wanted our five-year financial records, and various other things. And then they asked me to come up and have a meeting with them. That was in February 1986, and we consummated the deal in May of 1986.

I wanted cash, but now I am happy I did not sell for cash. They were very honest and said up front that they could not pay cash. It turned out to be an absolutely perfect marriage. They have kept me on as a consultant, and as a member of their board. It is a very well-run, and very wonderful, company.

□

Ken Poorman sold two data-processing companies to public companies in 1994. Total sales were $15+ million.

Hire a firm that specializes in this kind of thing to guide you through the process. These firms are expensive, but they package you so you present yourself in the most positive way, and secondly they really create a competitive environment which I think in the end results in a higher price–and they pay for themselves.

One was probably a textbook example of how pleasant it can be, and the other was probably a textbook example of how stressful it can be.

Sale of the two businesses involved two separate negotiations. One was probably a textbook example of how pleasant it can be, and the other was probably a textbook example of how stressful it can be. One's initial feelings about the people you are going to be negotiating with would tell you which category they are in. But hindsight's great.

It has worked out very well for us. We had over 200 employees, and every one of those people have jobs today. No one was fired. The culture with one of the companies has been very positive for the employees. The culture in the other company has not been as easy an adjustment, but still all those people have jobs–which was one of our goals.

One's initial feelings about the people you are going to be negotiating with would tell you . . .

My partner–who owned half the company, and I owned the other half–was ten years older than me, and he was really at a point when he wanted to retire. At that stage of my life I did not want to buy him out. The more we talked the more it came back to only one answer–sell to a third party. In a perfect world I would have wanted to hang in there maybe another five or ten years.

The top three issues for us were a balance among price, the well being of our employees, and the well being of our customers.

□

Harold Blumenkrantz sold a healthcare business (with revenues of about $25 million) in 1992 to a larger public company in the same field.

Judging from what happened with us, I would say the biggest problem is identifying the potential buyers. On my own I would not have come to the ultimate buyer in a thousand years. I didn't even know there was such a company.

Identifying the potential buyers is one of the biggest jobs. If you can do that on your own, that's fine. If not, obviously, having a broker is an important factor.

I wanted to have some very good years left . . .

One of the biggest issues is being prepared psychologically–to actually sell the business. I had a business that I thought was going to pass on to a member of my family, but that person said that he did not want to do this for the rest of his life.

I started trying to judge my own mortality. I realized that no one was going to buy my business unless I was willing to put in some time afterwards–and the longer I waited I still had a working period after the sale. I wanted to have some very good years left to do a lot of the things that I have talked about doing. That was another reason to sell, once my son wasn't interested. And, of course, the dollars weren't bad either.

The biggest change in my working life is that I earn a lot less money. Beyond that, not a damn thing, unfortunately. I am working just as hard as I ever did, doing everything the same. Having very little in the way of decisions that are being made for me. I really could wake up one day, and, if my paycheck were different, I would think I was doing what I did before. Nothing has changed, at this point.

. . . big companies take a long time to do everything . . .

The negotiations gave me an appreciation of the fact that big companies take a long time to do everything. I thought that the people we dealt with were exceedingly honest and forthright–forgetting that they wanted to buy whatever they could for the smallest amount, and we wanted the greatest amount. Apart from that, I was a little surprised at the honesty and integrity of the people we dealt with.

A top issue is getting the most that you can for what you sell.

> . . . the three-year employment contract . . . is a long time . . .

Secondly, although the three-year employment contract doesn't sound like an eternity, it is a long time, and I think it is very important that you have somebody you can live with for those years–otherwise, you can be an awfully miserable person. That would certainly be a big issue.

The third one would tie in with the second one, and that is the quality of the people who buy you. How they are going to ask you to run your business afterwards, because the business we sold is very personalized, and we would not want to have had to make any major changes with our customers.

□

Robert F. Kastelic made metal enclosures for electronic products, and sold in 1996. Sales were about $8 million, and the buyer was a public company.

My main concern in selling my business was the future of the employees and the business. I say that because we had gone through a number of hard times together, and developed some strong personal relationships. I wanted to find a buyer that was interested in keeping the organization together and providing an environment where the employees and the company could grow.

> . . . we had gone through a number of hard times together, and developed some strong personal relationships.

My second concern was to find a company with a good reputation and that had a somewhat similar philosophy–being people and employee oriented, and with some synergy or some strategic reason for getting into the metal fabrication business.

> . . . a tax-free exchange of stock, and so my investment in the buyer is gross of tax . . .

And, thirdly, the financial and tax ramifications for me as an individual were important. I sold for stock, and I wanted that. I wanted the stock of a company that I felt comfortable with, one I would be willing to invest in for several years. It was a tax-free exchange of stock–and so my investment in the buyer is gross of tax, and therefore substantially larger than if I had to pay taxes on the proceeds of the sale.

The negotiations were very simple. The chief executive and I sat down and agreed on an earnings multiple. I knew my financial statements very well, and I knew that there would not be any major adjustments or surprises because of the way I kept my books. I was able to come up with a figure, and I said, "Paul, that sounds fine to me. On that basis we can do it–let's bring the due diligence people in, and let them satisfy you that everything is fine."

> I spent ten years going through hell, and I want to get paid for that.

A number of sellers do not have a feel for the economic value of what they are selling–it's more an emotional value, feeling "Oh my God, I spent ten years going through hell, and I want to get paid for that." That's well and good that you spent ten years going through hell, but that does not make it any more valuable than the economics of the transaction. Period. They are what they are–regardless of how much of your blood sweat and tears went into it.

Looking back, I might have thought up a few other little twists on the financial side–nothing that significant. For example, the dollar price that we came up with was based on the average closing price of the stock for fifteen or thirty days prior to the final closing. Looking back, I would have done as well or better if I had said, "Let's fix it at the price of the stock on the day of the closing." It was not that significant: I am going to be in that stock for two years anyway, and it's going to go up and down in the course of two years, I am sure.

> . . . these rules require that I do not sell any shares for two years.

I am restricted from selling any shares for two years because of the accounting rules. The buyer wanted a pooling-of-interests [see page 164], and these rules require that I do not sell any shares for two years. What I can do, though, is go to Merrill Lynch, and say I want to do a transaction where you guarantee you will pay me 90% of today's market value, no matter what happens to the stock in the next two years; on the other side, I will give you any appreciation over 140% of today's price at the end of two years. Merrill Lynch said, "Yes, we could do that. Since we would have a floor on the price, a fixed guarantee, we could then find a lender who would advance money based on the guaranteed share price, and then we could reinvest those loans in other stocks to diversify your portfolio—this would hedge your position over that two-year period." All the brokerage firms do that—Bear Stearns, Merrill Lynch, Lehman Brothers. In fact when the notice went out that I had sold my company I must have gotten ten or twelve calls from different brokers saying, "We specialize in advising people who have restricted stock as to how to hedge their exposure."

□

2

Businesses Sold to Private Companies

Ron Marsilio made molded cable assemblies (sales around $20 million), and sold in 1993 to a larger company with related activities.

> If you have the luxury of market timing, I think it is critically important to have the trend line of–hopefully both–revenue and profit to be in a positive slope, rather than a flat slope or negative slope. Buyers have a tendency to be line extenders, and they'll pay you multiples on the extension of what they believe the trend lines are. And, much like trading stocks, I think it's important not to hold on to get the highest tick–once the tick turns down on you, you've essentially lost a lot more than if you sold a little bit early, when the momentum was still on the upside.

> Buyers have a tendency to be line extenders . . .

> It was clear that my company was moving along very strongly, and when we started negotiations we were still on an upswing so that the multiples they used were on a positive slope. The negative slope came after the closing. So I got very close to the peak of it, but had I waited even six months I probably would not have got the money that I got.

> . . . it is critically important to have more than one player . . .

I think it is critically important to have more than one player in during the negotiations. In addition to the obvious competitive nature of the bidding that might happen–although I don't encourage anyone to try to turn it into a bidding war–if people are aware that there are other people interested, small obstacles seem to get wiped out of the way fairly quickly, whereas if they are the only buyer negotiating you'll get stuck on little details for a protracted period of time. And I think what happens is that it starts extending the negotiating period, and the due diligence period–which is generally negative for the seller, and positive for the buyer. I found that having someone else there to keep it moving along was important.

We ended up getting three offers, and we had to sign a letter of intent with one of them. We had an offer, a letter of intent, that was going to expire–and we were going to take that deal, if we didn't get any other offers. We were meanwhile trying to encourage the others to make offers.

We took the second deal, but they always knew the first one was still there. Every time the negotiations started getting to the point where I could dig my heels in, their mind quickly went to the fact that I was sitting on another letter of intent from people who were disappointed that they did not get us. So it really moved it along–more than just trying to bid up the price, it put me in a throttling position on the speed of the thing, which was important.

A strategic buyer will ignore multiples, and ignore some downsides . . .

It is far better to pick a strategic buyer than it is to pick an investment buyer, in my opinion. Although sometimes an investment buyer is all you can get interested in the company at that time. A strategic buyer will ignore multiples, and ignore some downsides, if they think there is synergy.

A strategic buyer is obviously far better. If they think you can add something to their organization, or they can help your organization with things that they have, it helps a great deal.

They were very concerned about the continued management of the organization–and that made a post-closing deal for me very attractive.

It was a three-year, "no cut" contract, and I would recommend that to anyone staying on. It gets you out of the position where they can hire you for six months or so, pick your brain for everything, and terminate you summarily. In my employment agreement I could only be terminated for fraud or some other improper activity–it was not in any way tied to performance of the business.

The most important issue for a seller is timing the sale. Buyers want to look at financial statements for a couple of years to see the trend. You want to have the negotiations when the trend in sales and profit is positive.

I hope the other guy doesn't get it . . .

The second critical issue is to get one–or hopefully, more than one–strategic buyer involved. Have at least two buyers–it takes their mind away from, "Gee, are we sure we want to do this?" Instead, they think, "Gee, I hope the other guy doesn't get it." In that mindset, the buyer is a lot easier to deal with, and to move along more quickly.

Another important thing is to go through a preliminary due diligence on your own. We anticipated the buyer's due diligence, and did as much as we could in advance. It achieved three things: it suggested to the buyer that management was competent; it showed we were serious about our goal; and it allowed us to clean up some things before the buyer started worrying about them–and perhaps begin to wonder what else was wrong. We had our ducks in a row–we cleaned up paperwork, and wrote off some inventory. We took a small hit on the front end, before the due diligence got started.

□

Jonathan Dill made cylinders and sold in 1994 to a leveraged buyout firm that owned a related business. Sales were some $10 million.

I think it is important to find a synergistic buyer. They are clearly able and willing to pay more. They are looking to the future. A lot of times financial buyers buy the past, but a synergistic buyer can create a new and brighter future. So he'll pay more, and you can demand more, because it's worth more to him.

A lot of times financial buyers buy the past . . .

We looked at the industry. It was consolidating. It was either buy somebody to grow ourselves, or sell out and be associated with a bigger outfit. It is a very capital intensive business. We needed capital to expand, and to replace machinery. The family did not feel it was appropriate to put a lot of money into the company for capital investment or acquisitions, so it turned out to be a good thing to sell. The market timing was right. We were having a record year, and we were projecting a record year. We had a lot of things going for us. We looked around until we found a good synergistic buyer.

The buyer already owned a cylinder company. They wanted to grow that business very rapidly, and they wanted to add our company to theirs.

Negotiations were long. They literally took over a year. I was very honest up-front. We had a price, and we knew what we wanted. We wanted to sell the stock of our corporation rather than the assets. They asked what the price was. We told them. They figured this was a used car or someone selling a house: you ask one price, but you are willing to accept a lower price. They kept coming back, and we kept saying, "No, we are not interested. Get lost. That's the price." It took them about a year to understand that we were serious.

Meanwhile, our sales were growing, and our projections were coming true. We were doing quite well, and making good money. We were under no pressure to sell, other than the shareholders wanted to sell at some point. We did not have to sell that month, or even that particular year.

They figured this was a used car. . .

Finally, they realized the price was firm, and there was no more haggling about that. It made sense. It was fully priced, but it was not over-priced.

I'm still with the company, but the managers of their other company have decided not to use my capabilities. They required that the other key people and I be willing to stay with the company. They were buying management as much as anything, which I think was intelligent. They decided to keep the technical management, but, although I have a four-year employment contract, they have asked me to step aside, and be available if anyone wants to talk to me. Meanwhile, they are paying off on the contract, so I can't complain.

Top issues include the structure of the deal–tax considerations, whether or not you take notes, and everything else. A lot of people came to me who did not know much about making cylinders, and even some who didn't know much about manufacturing, and said, "Gee, I'd like to buy your business–would you take half the price in a long-term note?" You know, "Get lost."

What you are really looking for is how much money do you have left over when it is all said and done. A big consideration is taxes. The time value of money–all these things related to the structure are critical. We would have preferred stock for stock, but that was not available, so cash for stock was fine. Cash for assets was not acceptable–for tax reasons. One important thing for family-owned companies is the fate of the business. One of the criteria that we set up was that the business had to stay in Milwaukee, and everybody had to be employed by the buyer. They were willing to commit to this. It made sense to them. You have to keep in mind that the shareholders can take their money and leave, but what does it mean for all the people who helped them earn all that money?

You can accept a lower price if you have a better structure.

□

Robert DeLia made fiber optic communications products and sold in 1996 to a private company. Sales were about $13 million.

I've been through it a couple of times. It's something like a marriage. The first round I did was with a venture capital firm. And then I sold to a private company. It's not all money. It is the people you are going to have to live with after the deal is done–unless you are just going to cash out (then, "Who cares?" You go for bucks).

But if your intent is to stay, and work with the company, and make it grow, a little less money, but a better relationship, is much more important, in my mind.

It's not all money . . .

I couldn't tell you how many people I've discussed mergers and acquisitions with over 28 years. And there was a common thread amongst 95% of them–it was, "Gee, you've got a nice business, let us take it over, and we'll let you work harder to pay yourself back." And I'd scratch my head and say, "I must have straw hanging out of my mouth. Who needs you?" I could see if you were young and starting up with no experience, that's appealing–you've got nothing, and somebody comes in and gives you a sum of money and then you work yourself into the grave to make something out of it. They own it all, and give you nothing. That is one thing I would always look for–what kind of a deal are they offering? It tells you a lot about the people. How good they are.

The buyer appealed to me for several reasons. Number one was their attitude–and the way the company operated. Number two it would not hurt us in our market–we talked to some people in our industry and if we went with them some of our customers might have viewed us as competitors. This buyer was . . . ho, hum, who cared? It would enhance us, not hurt us.

. . . it would not hurt us in our business . . .

The people that I report to are realistic and generous. They've set goals–that's fine. I would expect that. Talking and working with them makes me feel that these guys are realists. They want us to work as hard as we can. I don't have a problem with that. But, on the other hand, they are real. They know enough about the industry to know it goes through ups and downs–and it does. They are in touch with what we do. The organization seems smooth. They put a lot of stock in people. It's not all profits.

The negotiations were horrible. I just felt that negotiations like that should not be adversarial–they should be more like dating. Should be. But. . . . that's behind us.

I think it is time we find people who have already walked this trail . . .

My prime concern was the company's future growth. I thought we could grow on our own. The company was stable, profitable–we had all the things in place. But, with a little more horsepower, and the experience of people who have been there, we could achieve our goals a lot faster. Every step we took was like walking in a mine field. None of us here have that much experience. I was saying I think it is time to find people who have already walked this trail, and let them help us—save us a few steps.

Number two in my mind was finding a company that would leave us intact, because a lot of people put a lot of blood, sweat, and tears into this place, and they weren't stockholders. I didn't want to see this place get torn apart. And that was my second largest issue.

Third was money.

□

Jack Parlog made graphics products for electronic components and sold in 1994 to a private company. Sales were about $16 million.

It's a very painstaking process that you go through. First of all, you have to make sure that you want to sell the business. You have to understand why it is that you want to sell the business. I think these things have to be very, very clearly understood before entering into any discussions or taking any steps in the process. As a business owner or manager, you are involved in the day-to-day operations and the care and nurturing of your people, your products, and you're involved with the growth of the business. When it comes to the actual process of selling the business, most people are unprepared for it. There are so many aspects, nuances if you will, in the actual negotiation and sale of the business, and you are just not prepared for it, unless you have done it before.

Good counsel, experienced in mergers and acquisitions, helps, but even with that, there is just so much—so many different things that have to be examined, and weighed. Even with good counsel, you think you understand, but you don't until it's all finalized. Hopefully, if you are dealing with the right people, everything turns out to everyone's benefit in the end.

> . . . most people are unprepared . . .

The key is dealing with the right people. You first have to decide why you want to sell, then it is equally important to try to identify who would be the ideal buyer, that would carry on things that you feel are important.

There are many different reasons why people want to sell a business–they want to do other things, for estate planning . . . a whole variety of reasons for selling. In our particular situation, I felt that the acquisition of our company–it was and is a very successful operation–would let us be better poised for future operations if we had substantial financial backing. The sale of the company was in the best interests of the company and the employees that built this company.

As I look back at the negotiations, and as I was going through it, there were just so many small details that had to be addressed by both buyer and seller. And of course the buyer is the one who is bringing up many of these small details. The buyer of our company was very experienced in acquisitions, and this was my first go at it.

In our situation it was an unsolicited approach to our company, but once discussions took place with the buyer, and once we saw their background, their diversity and financial strength, it began to make a lot of sense for the company for the long term.

Looking back, I would take further advantage of counsel to understand some things that perhaps I didn't have a real clear concept of at the time. There are certain formulae involved that are tied to the performance. At the time, I thought I understood, but very honestly my understanding was not as clear as it should have been. This is a minor issue compared to the overall transaction. Certainly, everything we do in life, if we take a look back, we could probably have done it a little bit better in one aspect or another. I am extremely satisfied with the transaction overall.

Top three issues for a seller . . . one, be sure why you want to sell–I think that is extremely important because you have to have it well thought out. As there is buyer's remorse, I am sure also that there is something called seller's remorse–and it would be a sad thing to experience.

Understanding the real value of the company, and how to determine it, is fundamental. Then, finding the right buyer is key. In our situation, the right buyer found us. We had been approached many, many times in the past, but in this situation it was the right buyer–it made sense for the company, for the future growth of the company, as well as the owners of the company.

Making sure that you want to sell—and the reasons for that decision—is number one.

□

Jack Byrne was president of a small publicly-owned specialty chemical company in the late 1970's. Sales were $10+ million. It was acquired in 1978 by a private company with $200+ million in sales.

I'd advise a seller first to get his store in order. Put together a strategic plan for the next three or five years, so that he can demonstrate to the buyer what he has, and the potential.

I think it is very important how you package the business. We did a real good job because we were professionally managed: we were a public company at the time so we had good reporting, good internal controls, etc.

The top three people are still in place 15 years after the closing. That's an endorsement of the marriage. Had we been acquired by a *Fortune* 500 company, there is no way that the top management would still be here. The culture of the private company that acquired us, and their strategy—that is to let us continue to run our own businesses, with an incentive plan based on growth and autonomy—just made a lot of sense for the cast of characters that were here. Being part of a private company, we did not have the quarter-to-quarter earnings issues, and things like that.

> . . . it is very important how you package the business.

As president and CEO of a public company, I reported to a board of directors, and this same arrangement continued with the new owner. That is unusual.

Our financial people had huge burdens—at least they described them as huge burdens—to start off with, but then I think common sense prevailed and we were able to scale that back.

We were negotiating with two public companies, and the private company came in late—but they acted quickly. They made an offer for the company three weeks after our first meeting, and the deal closed about two months later.

> They didn't dictate how we should run the business. They listened to us.

Autonomy was a key factor in the success of our marriage. They didn't dictate how we should run the business. They listened to us. They gave us financial support. They left us alone. And that is where I think the large public companies would have failed. Look at the history–the large chemical companies acquired flavor and fragrance companies, and I'll bet that 80% of them destroyed the businesses. Pharmaceutical companies acquired cosmetics companies, and they just smothered them.

The success of the business helped. When you are making the great numbers that we were, it is very easy to be a bit arrogant, and say you don't want anyone to bother you. If results had been a roller coaster, the relationships would have been different, and I doubt if the three guys would still be here.

□

Bill Cash was a principal in a healthcare business sold in 1992. Revenues were $24 million. The buyer was a private company with related businesses.

Sellers need to decide what their motivation is–do I need a partner? Am I going to stay? Do I go completely? How does it affect me personally?

> What kind of value-added can these purchasers bring?

Most purchasers want you to stay around at least in the short run to make the transition, especially in a technical business. And some businesses are not worth nearly as much without the principal.

I made some errors. You need to know who you are dealing with. You need to decide about the character of the people you are dealing with. Can you trust them? And I think you need to do a lot of reference checking, a lot of reference checking, about the people that you are considering selling to.

> . . . the promises turn to dust.

It is like a marriage. During the dating period, there are roses and everything's nice. As soon as the courtship is over, all the promises turn to dust. So I think it is real, real critical that you understand who you are dealing with, and to get a track record–to call other people who have been through this experience with those purchasers.

There was another party that talked to us right after we had signed the letter of intent who would have offered us public stock, and that would have given people their liquidity–as opposed to a payday some day.

All-cash deals tend to drive the price down . . .

The price is critically tied to the terms. All-cash deals tend to drive the price down, cash with terms mean that you can probably get a higher price–perhaps with earn-outs, earnings hurdles, whatever.

You need to ask, "What kind of value-added can these purchasers bring?" That is where I really made my mistake. I thought our buyer's people really could bring something to the table, and, honestly, if you put it on a balance, they actually took away, as opposed to adding.

I think there are deals out there that are synergistic. If it is just money, maybe that is not a good reason to do the deal. I think there needs to be something more, either in the form of expertise, or contacts, or related business, or putting two companies together to make a stronger third one, or something.

Other things I would do differently are I would be careful about noncompete agreements: I would make sure there is a clear exit. If you get mostly all cash up front, fine–then be willing to be tied down to a noncompete. But if you don't get all cash up front, then I would arrange maybe non-solicitation, but not noncompete. Sellers need to understand the difference between non-solicitation, and noncompete.

I lost control of probably 30% of my day . . .

I was introduced to the buyer by a friend. Interestingly enough, late in the process he called and said, "Be careful."

After the new buyers came in, I lost control of probably 30% of my day . . . reporting this, reporting that, statistical this, statistical that. . . . It had a lot to do with teaching the new people about the business. Some of this is valuable, some of it is not.

If you have several classes of shareholders, perhaps somebody with a majority, and a group of minority shareholders, I would make sure that everybody is on the same page. If you treat shareholders differently, it creates a lot of ill will during the negotiations–and it may eventually hurt the company.

□

Bill Axelrod sold a maker of disc-brake parts to a large private company in the 1980's. Sales were some $3 million.

It was not an auction. I was looking for a specific relationship–different from one I had had earlier selling a business to a public corporation.

This time we were acquired by a private corporation–which made all the difference in the world. You don't have a four-inch book of policies that you have to adhere to. And you don't have two or three people from the corporate office overseeing your every move. When you have been a family business, this change is very difficult.

With a private company the entrepreneurship becomes the important factor, and you are given an opportunity to continue to do what they liked when they bought you.

This time we were acquired by a private corporation–which made all the difference in the world.

After the closing the business grew very rapidly, and we were given the opportunity to expand at will to take care of the opportunities that were available–shortage of capital had limited us before.

If you have confidence in the broker, and he has experience putting together companies of different types, he can relax you in the relationships that you develop between buyer and seller–and then you have someone extremely valuable in putting the package together. The Selling Memorandum was important because it told a little bit of the story of the company–where it had been and what the potential was. The broker did a big job screening people before introducing them to us–this was important: otherwise, a lot of time is wasted, and it creates a burden.

People issues are as important as the financial issues.

□

Woody Comstock sold several businesses in the late 1980's when he restructured a public company with sales of about $40 million. The businesses–with sales from $2 million to $18 million–made various products, from electric motors to parts for pianos. The buyers were individuals and private companies.

The first thing you have to do is establish a value. It basically comes down to certain multiples that are recognized in the financial marketplace. I would try to establish a value that the individual needed in his own mind, which then could be related to something that was understood in the general economic market. A strategic buyer may pay more. That could be a supplier, someone downstream–a customer, or a competitor–someone who understood the market, so a lot of the sales work is already done.

I would rather settle in with one, or at most, two . . .

The easiest one for us, and the largest, was the sale of a piano keys and actions business, where the market was changing radically. We just went to the biggest guy in the marketplace and said, "We have been supplying you for a hundred years–you really ought to do this yourself, so that you control the process." We convinced them that they should control what was probably their single largest outside purchase, in dollars. It became relatively easy then.

A lot of people say you ought to have twenty people competing against each other, but I am not an advocate of that. I would rather settle in with one, or at most two, people that you thought were the most likely to be successful, and try to drive something out of them.

With a small business, it is not always possible to generate lots of buyers. It is particularly bothersome if your first negotiations fall apart, and if you have in advance spread it out to twenty people. I think you are at a disadvantage going back later to the other nineteen.

If you are going to split the difference, let the other guy tell you that.

If the individual selling can possibly do it, I would slow down the process. There is a lot given up just in timing, "We've got to do this, we've got to do that." The next thing you know, you've given away a million dollars. Sometimes guys get to the point when they are apart–whether it is one dollar or a million dollars–where somebody will inevitably say, "Let's split the difference." If you are going to split the difference, let the other guy tell you that. So that he has already come up half-way, then you have the advantage of being able to say, "I can't quite do that–but if you toss in another $100,000, we'll do it." So if the gap were one million dollars, now you've got $600,000 instead of $500,000. Pace is important.

You've got to understand who is buying, and their capability–it's one thing to sell something to IBM, and another to sell something to an individual. You have to understand their capacity to buy.

Keep the process focused, I think, on one or two guys. It has got to have a pace, but not so frantic that you leave money on the table.

. . . you want to cut the rope, and be done . . .

Price is obviously the number one issue–but the baggage you take with you after the price may be more important. When you sell it, you want to cut the rope and be done–and we have not always been successful at this, and that is why it is poignant for me. You don't want any liabilities remaining, you don't want any reps and warranties that go on forever, because they'll always bite you. There is always something, even in the cleanest deal, as honest and open as you may be. Since you've made that decision to get out of it, the sooner and the cleaner it can be done, the better. Make sure the price is whole, so you don't have all those reps and warranties hanging over you.

□

Marvin Levine sold an institutional pharmacy with sales of about $8 million in 1993 to a private company in the same business.

Get a broker. I have sold two businesses through brokers. The advantages of selling through a broker are that you have a much broader market, and you get a more valid evaluation of what the business is worth because of the broker's exposure to many buyers.

I don't think you need legal help until towards the end of the process, although I did get preliminary accounting help to help me assess whether to sell stock or assets. An overriding issue for the first business that I sold was licenses held by the corporation–and selling the assets rather than the corporation would have meant the buyer would be without licenses for a while.

Doctor, don't treat yourself. . .

Having the buffer of a partial negotiator, the broker, who wants to make the deal, is very, very important because he can feel out the emotional climate. He can make a more realistic evaluation of the feelings of both buyer and seller. "Doctor, don't treat yourself. Lawyer, don't represent yourself." You want some unemotional involvement. The broker can be a kind of referee.

I had no pressing need to sell. I was at a point where it would be a good idea to sell, but I had a fallback position–to sell it over time to a key employee.

The changes in my working life with a new owner were not as anticipated. Many friends have the same situation. I thought I was going to be operating exactly as I had before, but in a corporate environment. Changes in the hierarchy of the buying company led to changes in my role.

. . . you should feel at least 60–40 in favor of selling . . .

The top three issues are, to be able to achieve in the sale a minimum of five times your yearly income; comfort in realizing that this is what you want to do–you should feel at least 60–40 in favor of selling. And be realistic: you may not get what you expect, but you should rely on the referee, the broker, that this is what it is worth.

. . . you will not have the same interest and enthusiasm . . .

I thought I would like to continue to work the way I used to. It didn't turn out that way, and I am glad that it didn't. No matter what you think at the time you sell, if you have been running your own company for years, you will not have the same interest and enthusiasm. It just isn't so. I am very happy with the way it worked out. I am contributing somewhat, and I have some place to go–and that was an overriding consideration. If you have worked all your life, you need some place to go in the morning. I didn't want to sit around and wait for something to happen. Its 90% less stressful. But a certain amount of stress is desirable–it's interesting.

□

Jack McChord was a principal in a medical equipment company sold in 1987. It had sales of about $10 million.

First of all, I would tell a seller that it is a natural feeling that there is no good time to sell. People often say, "Not right now; I am not ready to quit." But there probably never is a good time, an ideal time.

> . . . it is a natural feeling that there is no good time to sell . . .

First and foremost, find a good partner: someone who is compatible. If you are one of the principals that stays around, as I was, you fight a continual battle of the "we-versus-they" mentality. Original employees worry that the people from the new parent might rip out all the plants in the front lobby–they are always looking for some nefarious plot.

> . . . people from the new parent might rip out all the plants in the front lobby . . .

Meet with your counterpart in the other company and forge an agreement with him, so that the spirit of the agreement carries through when the attorneys and others start nit-picking. Form a relationship with the top guy to establish the spirit of a relationship–and even when he is not there in subsequent meetings you can bring up that agreement.

Seek the advice of professionals.

The paper outweighs you.

Talk to people who were acquired by the same buyer.

> . . . did not want to go to the local supermarket and find former employees bagging groceries . . .

I can look former employees in the eye without concern. I was worried about that: I did not want to go to the local supermarket and find former employees bagging groceries, thinking I got a bundle.

Maintain secrecy. Get it done quickly. We got it done in 60 days. You are not doing other things you should be doing; employees get nervous. Watch your reps and warranties.

□

Jim Schill sold a processor of chemicals for the rubber and plastics industries to a private company in 1995. Sales were over $25 million.

The easiest way is to just go to a business broker, or you can go to a major accounting firm. In my own situation I chose to seek out logical buyers and talk to them personally because we had two objectives–the company was owned by seven shareholders: my partner and I owned 37.5% apiece, and the other 25% was owned by five individuals. Jack and I had reached retirement age. The company had been quite successful, and when we first formed it the intent was to have the other shareholders buy us out, but the value of the company had reached a point where they could not borrow enough from banks, because banks are not interested in lending on goodwill. Much of the value of our company was in the goodwill because of the very successful growth rate we had–about 20% compounded.

We opted to handle it ourselves.

I was interested in getting a good price, but I was also interested in making certain that whoever bought the company would treat the people fairly. A lot of our customers had been purchased, and, in our experience, after the buyer pays a very satisfactory price, the owner leaves happy but then the buyer tries to recoup a lot of the selling price out of the hide of the people who are left behind–massive layoffs, limitations on wage increases, sometimes even reductions in wages, reductions in bonuses, reductions in fringe benefits–and then it becomes an unsuccessful purchase because all the good people leave out of resentment. The buyer is left with what nobody else wants, and then his purchase becomes a failure. And in many instances they don't comprehend why.

We wanted to be certain that our people would be left to do their thing the way they had been doing it all along. And I didn't feel that a broker, who is interested in finding a buyer as quickly as he can, because he is going to get a certain percentage of the selling price . . . his concern is not for the people who are left behind. His concern is for how quickly he can make a deal. We opted to handle it ourselves. It depends on the individual. Not everyone wants to do that.

Buyers all seem to feel they are at a fire sale . . .

The key is finding someone who is interested in your company for what it is. Someone who does not look at it and say, "How can we dismember this thing?" thinking that old saying, the individual parts are worth more than the whole. Given a preference, we would choose a private company as a buyer. Our issue was who was going to pay a fair price, and treat us right. And it wouldn't have mattered to me who that was. We did have discussions with ten or twelve people, some of whom were private, and some of whom were public.

A lot of the prospective buyers thought five times earnings was a fair price . . .

I did find, frankly, that there is a reluctance to pay what I consider to be a fair price. Buyers all seem to feel they are at a fire sale–you would not be selling if you were not quite desperate to get out. So they make what I consider ridiculous offers. I keyed our asking price to the S&P Industrials price-earnings ratio, which at the time was in the neighborhood of 15 or 16 times earnings. That's an after-tax multiple, and generally when you are talking about selling a business you are talking about pretax earnings–I would convert the 15-16 by multiplying it by 0.6 and that would put you in the range of 9-10 times the pretax earnings. And that is what we thought was a fair price. A lot of the prospective buyers thought five times earnings was a fair price–especially when they were depending on their banks. We were talking to a number of people who themselves had bought the companies not too long prior to our talks, through management buyouts and so forth, and in those instances the bank would always come with a proposition that involved five times earnings. I considered that an insulting offer.

We did not have a prospectus. We would send a one-page letter describing the business, describing the results, and there were charts. I suppose you could call it a very informal prospectus. That was simply to get their attention. We would mention our compounded growth rate, but on the initial go-around we did not want to be too specific because we ourselves were a private company and we felt the more information we gave out the more detrimental it would be. For instance, we never gave financial information to Dun & Bradstreet–I've always felt that is simply educating your competitors. I was reluctant to put too much in the hands of prospective buyers until the time we had a signed confidentiality agreement. After that we were pretty open with them.

Most of the prospective buyers were major raw material suppliers. We considered them the logical purchasers for our business. In essence, we were taking those raw materials and putting them through a value-added process, and then selling them. We were one of the largest consumers in the country of rubber chemicals, especially rubber accelerators. In essence, we were a funnel–the suppliers used to sell to 40 or 50 companies, but we went in and converted these people to using our products, and now the suppliers sold just as many chemicals but to one company. It rechanneled the distribution.

Some of our suppliers had told us that they would be interested in working out some kind of an arrangement with us–joint ventures, mergers, or something of that sort. And they were interested in doing this overseas–we were primarily selling domestically. And these were the people we knew the best. We were in contact with them daily. It was like talking to friends and acquaintances.

The ultimate buyer was not a supplier of ours. This company approached us through a broker. The broker simply served as an intermediary to introduce us. I never met the broker. We exchanged several letters. The buyer had contacted the broker and told him of their interest in prospective acquisitions. The buyer took over the contact after the broker conveyed information about our business.

. . . lawyers are not wont to do that . . .

The top two issues for a seller are price, and how is the buyer going to treat the company after they own it. And the third is probably proper legal representation–you have these lengthy discussions and you have your own conception of what has been agreed to. You think that you and the buyer are in common accord, but somebody has to draw up the instruments and in this instance the attorneys for the buyer drew them up. I already had a relatively low regard for the legal profession–I think anybody in business comes out with a low regard for the legal profession. One of the things I had said to the buyer was "Let's make sure that the lawyers simply put down what we agree to." But lawyers are not wont to do that–lawyers are being retained by somebody, and they always feel that they have to give that somebody an edge. So if the other fellow is drawing up the papers, you have to be very certain that your lawyer really looks them over and makes sure that your interests are represented fairly. The way I feel about it, if the instruments are drawn up fairly, you can sign them from either side of the table–if you are the buyer you can sign them, and if you are the seller you can sign them. They shouldn't give any kind of an advantage to either side, other than exactly what you agreed on. I think that an important third issue is to have proper and experienced legal representation.

□

Frank Consalvo sold a maker of access control products to a private company in 1994. Sales were $45 million.

Make sure you understand the kind of buyer you want to obtain. It's not like putting a house on the market, and looking for a qualified buyer, one with money. I think when you sell a business, especially one that you have founded or invested in, and have an ongoing commitment to, even after you sell it, you need to know your buyer.

> You can profile a buyer just as you might profile a new employee.

You can profile a buyer just as you might profile a new employee. There are certain characteristics that you would like to identify, including integrity, commitment to the field that you have invested in, the same philosophical approach to employees–those kinds of qualities.

I have been involved in four different companies over the years. And the first one was Sony Corporation. I was with an electronics company and we wanted to be acquired. None of us were over 30, and none of us had any real experience, but we profiled the conditions that we wanted. We had substantial offers from much larger companies–at that time Sony Corporation was $70 million. It had all the characteristics we wanted, and we pursued it–we hadn't even been approached by them. And it seemed to me that it fit so well I just followed that course of action.

> . . . they are more concerned with the relationships that exist within the company . . . than they are necessarily with the financial success. One is not a substitute for the other–it is just a matter of emphasis.

The companies that I have been involved in have been somewhat relational, and the investors and people have also been relational–they are more concerned with the relationships that exist within the company, and with suppliers and shareholders, than they are necessarily with the financial success. One is not a substitute for the other–it is just a matter of emphasis.

The top three issues are: a qualified buyer, price, and a sustained commitment to employees.

□

Jim Hall sold a remanufacturer of component parts for transmissions in 1988 to a private company; sales were $40 million.

I never had the business for sale. A broker that I had known in Ohio called and wanted to come in and talk to me, and for about a year I kind of ignored it, and then I guess I did it originally as kind of a favor to him.

> . . . just had gotten tired of the race . . .

They came in, and I got to thinking about it. It was time for us to do it. My brother and I owned it, and our families had gotten larger, and we were looking at a potential retained earnings problem.

We bought a lot of companies over the years and just had gotten tired of the race, I guess. We decided it would be a good time to get everybody in the families set.

> I guess you kinda scotch yourself from rolling back.

It has been a good situation. It has worked, and it did what we wanted it to do. The tax structure probably affected us more than anything. We had decided not to continue our growth–or not to expand and take chances, as we had done for all the years we had been in business. We wanted to settle down, but we realized a company has to grow–it can't just stay put. The tax structure was such that we were paying lots of taxes. We had nothing to depreciate. Historically, we had always purchased companies and maneuvered to gain market share and profits. With the tax structure as it is, after you get to a certain point you don't really gain anything. You face an estate tax, so why fight it and gamble. I guess you kinda scotch yourself from rolling back.

I have no ownership now. We did a cash sale. I've continued to run the business for seven years. And my brother continued for six years. And we are in other businesses, also–unrelated to the transmission parts business. We had those prior to selling the business.

The people came in and did an evaluation. And we did one, and we were very close together. We didn't haggle or anything. We had made the decision that it would be beneficial for us to go ahead and accept it.

I have sold a lot of businesses, and this has been the only one that I have ever been involved in that the philosophy that was talked about during the negotiations was carried through.

. . . the management attempts to make something better . . .

I have a lot of friends that have sold companies–almost without failure, the management attempts to make something better. And the philosophy of the group we sold to is that they just want a good solid company. For instance, if you have got somebody that over the years maybe they are now earning more than they are worth–their philosophy is if it is running good, making money, don't screw around with it.

Top three issues . . . You always have a feeling for the people. In my case, I started the company, so you kinda have a feeling for the company that you don't have if you are hired as a general manager, or CEO of an existing company. Of course, the price. And continuity–which very seldom happens.

□

"John Doe" sold a graphics business to a private company in 1996. Sales were about $15 million.

The most important thing to me is who you are getting in bed with. You must make sure that the people you are getting in bed with are credible, they are real, and they are of high moral character.

It's just like a marriage . . .

It's just like a marriage–you just want to make sure you are getting in bed with the right person. That would be the most sage advice I could give.

What sticks in my mind is the intense due diligence that came after the negotiations. The due diligence was extremely difficult–it was much more than I thought it was going to be. I didn't understand that I was going to have to give up my regular job in order to do due diligence.

. . . I was going to have to give up my regular job to do due diligence . . .

In terms of the negotiations, I told them what I wanted, and their immediate response was, "If you can prove to me that your numbers are true, that deal is makable." And that's what the due diligence was–to prove that what I had told them was real. We really didn't negotiate–because I had told them in no way, shape or form would I ever sell my business.

. . . he asked if I had seen *Indecent Proposal.*

I'll tell you the one thing that I thought was interesting about the negotiations. A gentleman–a broker from California–called me eleven times and I did not return any of his calls. Finally, I called him back: he said, "I bet you're wondering why I called." I said, "I am not wondering at all why you called–I called you because I want to offer you a job." He said, "You don't understand, I'm calling to buy your business." I said, "Sir, you don't understand–my business is not for sale, but I would like to hire you because anyone who can make eleven phone calls without ever getting a call returned is the type of guy that could sell for me." He laughed and said, "Why is your business not for sale." I said, "Because I am 45 years old, I have enough money to live on for the rest of my life, and I am absolutely not interested in this deal whatsoever." And he asked me if I had ever seen the movie *Indecent Proposal*. And I said, "Yes." He said, "So, in other words, if I offered you $200 million for your business you would have no interest." I said, "I didn't say that." He said, "Well, fine, then it's only price we are negotiating." So, basically, that was the whole play, which was the indecent proposal. There is a price for everything. Obviously at $200 million the answer would be yes. If the question was 84 cents the answer would be no–somewhere in between lies a number. And that is where the conversation started. That is probably the one part of the negotiations that sticks in my mind the most. Once I came up with a number, the buyer only asked me to prove it was worth it. And that is what due diligence did.

We signed our letter of intent in January, and we went through 90 days of intense due diligence–pretty unusual for a $15-million-sales company, based on comparisons that I have heard. We did not have audited financial statements–they brought in their own accountants, who, in essence, audited our financial statements. Our statements were reviewed by a public accounting firm.

Looking back, I would not have done anything differently.

I interviewed people who had sold to them. . .

The top three issues for a seller . . . Money, obviously. . . . My position in the remaining business–because I wanted to be a part of my baby in the future. And the third issue, who am I getting in bed with? I called the presidents of other companies that they had acquired–asked them about their deal, and how it had worked–not the economics, but what kind of people are these. I checked it out with people who had dealt with them before. I interviewed people who had sold to them.

□

3

Businesses Sold to Investors

James Robinson sold to an individual investor a light metal fabrication business with sales of $13 million late in 1993. The company made harness and saddlery hardware for horses, advertising display racks, floral wire baskets, and hardware for stoves and ranges.

> My company had sales of about $13 million, about 200 employees, and it had been in the family for about 90 years.
>
> Through the years I had kept a file of people who were making overtures, and I am sure a lot of them were fishing expeditions, and there really wasn't interest . . . people can get lists from Dun & Bradstreet. . . . I had a big file about an inch and a half thick that I had collected over the years. One of the things of course is to pick your time, if possible, when the company is in good financial shape . . . and the owner is still in relatively good health.
>
> Another thing: don't be too eager to sell. Consider all the options. One option is not to sell at that particular time.
>
> Pick someone in the company as a confidant who stands to gain from the sale. You just can't do it by yourself–you've got to have someone you can talk to and who can help you gather information, and can

keep it quiet. Pick someone who stands to gain–in my own case over the years I had sold about 16% of the stock to key people at half of the then existing book value–and when this fellow came along, he paid about 150% of book, so some of them stood to gain four, five, six, or seven times their original investment. And particularly the fellow I picked to be my confidant–it was my vice-president and general manager, and he stood to gain considerably from it. It helps to have all of your key people gain financially from the sale so they won't try to torpedo the transaction.

. . . make sure he is not a competitor in disguise . . .

Another thing, be careful to determine the real interest of any prospect before allowing him to sign a confidentiality agreement, and then showing him your books and records, and exposing your customer list and all those types of things. Make sure it is not just a fishing expedition–make sure he's not a competitor in disguise.

A friend of mine at the YMCA here in Chattanooga said to me one day, "Say Jim, did you ever think of selling?" And I said "No, I am 64 years old and in good health, but what do you have in mind?" He said he knew someone up in Hendersonville, Tennessee, who had some experience in turning companies around. I said my company is in the best shape it has ever been in, and it did not need turning around. He said well this person was now looking for a business which he could nurture for himself and his family. And that is how these things happen. He was not a hunter–not a paid hunter.

When it comes down to signing that letter of intent, I think it is absolutely essential that you pick a law firm as an advisor that has a good track record in sales of businesses. If you just pick your own lawyer, unless he knows what he is doing in this area, you can get ripped up quite readily.

Before you make your announcement to your employees, and the newspaper, you better be very, very sure that the prospect is financially capable of completing the deal. We signed this letter of intent way back in October, and it wasn't until December 27th that he finally worked out all of his arrangements with the banks and financial institutions–and in that time there were big questions in the eyes of a lot of our employees. "Is it really going to go through or not?" Make sure the guy can swing it–before you open up all your books and records. A lot of things fall through the cracks. In my particular case, with a closely held corporation, I wanted to pick someone as the prospective buyer who would carry on many of the corporate and family traditions–and not strip it of people, or its cash, and then sell it, or close it. Temperament, particularly, I think, is so very, very important. I wanted someone who would more or less carry it along like I had carried it all these 40 years.

If you sell to a large corporation very often what will happen is they will say, "Hmm, I don't think we need that sales organization down there. We'll just handle that out of headquarters up here." So that is sucked out. And then they say, "Hmm, I don't think we need that engineering function down there." So that's sucked out. "Hmm, I don't think we need that credit operation–we'll just take that, and let it be handled at headquarters up here." So, pretty soon, all you've got is just a manufacturing facility, and it is not the free-standing entity that it was, that you worked for all those years.

As far as the valuation is concerned, I found it very helpful to have somebody from the outside, with no ax to grind, help to evaluate the company. In my particular case, the only outside board member I had was the vice-president of finance for a large corporation with $2 billion in sales, and he was very knowledgeable about buying and selling companies. He was able to help me to evaluate this thing in about four different directions so that I could come up with something that was plausible.

> . . . let the buyer know very early on about what price range you are thinking of . . .

My next piece of advice would be to let the buyer know very early on about what price range you are thinking of. If it is somewhere in the neighborhood of one-and-a-half times the book value, tell him way up front so you do not have a lot of discussions that turn out to be fruitless.

Once it looks like the prospect is very, very serious, convert that vague figure of one-and-a-half times book value to a dollar amount, and stick to it. Don't have it tied to 1.5 times the book value because very often you will get tied up in a great argument as to the values of inventory and receivables, et cetera–and it is a continual argument. But if you say you want $7 million, or $8 million, stick with that number right there, and that eliminates a lot of fruitless hassle.

Of course, sell for cash if you possibly can, and the sale of your shares in your company is a whole lot better than a sale of the assets. An asset sale benefits the buyer. The seller is left with a lot of clouds hanging over him–it could be in the area of environmental violations, and settling up all the liabilities like purchases, pensions, healthcare bills, and a whole lot of other things. If you sell your shares outright you are out from under all that.

> . . . I found out in the fine print that I was going to be behind the bank . . .

If you are going to help to finance the deal with some sort of separate note, make sure it is adequately collateralized, but then be darn sure that you are not subordinated to a financial lending institution. Almost at the last minute, I was going to take a note for $1 million to kind of help move the thing along. There were about 38 acres of excess land that I was going to take as collateral on that note, but then I found out in the fine print that I was going to be behind the bank–if there were any violations of the covenants in the agreement that the purchaser had with the bank, he could be held in default, and then I was not going to get anything on my $1 million note. I would not even get paid interest on the note, much less the principal. So, make sure that you are not subordinated to the lending institution if you take a separate note.

Another thing. Make sure there is a statement in the sales agreement that there are no agents or commissions involved. And make sure that there are none hanging there in the wings, and not have someone say, "Hey, Jim, I was the one who put you two guys together, right–I think you ought to give me 5% of that sale." Make sure that is in the sales agreement.

Be sure that the buyer does not include in the purchase price any value on your noncompete agreement. If he assigns any value in that purchase price to the noncompete agreement, then I would have had to pay taxes on that.

Try to find someone whose temperament fits the organization, otherwise he will just tear it apart, and you'll have very unhappy people who have been serving you faithfully for years and years. They'll be leaving, and be unhappy, and they'll take it out on you.

In your announcement to your employees, try to keep it upbeat, optimistic and encouraging–and tell them that you are stepping aside so as not to hold up the company's progress and growth with old outdated ideas and traditions. The tendency for some people is to say, "He took his money and ran with it–and bailed out. He let us down." Say it will be "bigger and better, and go further than it ever did under my leadership. You won't be saddled with all the old traits and traditions and outmoded ideas that I had, so go with the fellow and run with it."

We had numerous meetings with the buyer. I got to know him pretty well. I also got a sense from other people who talked to him. My general manager and I talked to him first, and then other key people. My vice president of sales looked him over. And I brought in my outside director and he interviewed him. The consensus of opinion that came through in all these interviews was that this guy is solid, this guy is genuine, he is straight and up-front with us. We never caught him hedging the truth or circumventing anything. It was all very forthright.

I felt I was giving up my child for adoption. . .

I felt I was giving up my child for adoption to somebody who is really going to take care of it, and love it and nurture it–and do better, and go further than I was able to do.

Looking back, I would have made more effort to be sure that the guy could swing the deal financially before I signed the letter of intent, before I announced it to the newspapers and my employees. It was a long period of time from October to December, and a lot of questions arose. People did not know what their future was. And I did not know. People were just unsettled. Get satisfied early on.

□

Arthur Hilsinger sold a manufacturer of optical accessories in 1993 to an investment firm. Sales were about $17 million.

Some people don't know whether they want to leave. When they come up against that wall, they cannot do it. The emotional content in these decisions is huge.

I could not generalize about what advice I would give to someone. I think mostly I would discuss it with him in some depth. If he were in a situation like mine, the first decision to make would be whether to seek a strategic buyer or a financial buyer. Strategic being someone in the industry or with some business related to the industry. If there were reasons that the price could be leveraged up by selling to a strategic buyer, then I would certainly suggest that that would be the first place to go. A sale to a strategic buyer will generally get you more money.

The emotional content in these decisions is huge . . .

If there were reasons not to seek a strategic buyer, and in my case there were reasons I did not want to do a strategic sale, then I think–depending on the quality of the business being sold–you should try to get the appropriate financial buyer. And by appropriate I mean people who buy businesses of a similar type–and are especially interested in businesses of your size.

In my particular case, I have a niche business, and a strategic buyer might have tried to integrate this into one of the main line businesses in our industry, and I have been in the main line businesses in our industry, and I knew that would not work–I had to separate myself from it in the first place to build a successful niche business.

You have to think of what your view is about the people you have in your business. I have built a team of people over a number of years–over 35-40 years–and it is very important to me that they come out well on the deal, and that the company isn't folded up and they are put out of jobs. You have to weigh in your equation how much emphasis you want to put on keeping the business where it is, as opposed to moving it somewhere. Certain buyers, almost by definition, are going to want to move it. Others will not.

We were fortunate in that our business had been quite successful and we had a large number of high-quality people interested. We had 12-15 people who were very interested and that we talked seriously with. We were able to narrow it down to some *quality* financial buyers–and there are a lot out there that aren't.

A lot depends on your choices. Sometimes there is only one company that is interested in you, and then, if you want to sell, you've got to figure out how to do it with them. We were fortunate in that we had a number, and the outstanding thing is that the people that we finally sold the business to were very straightforward, and they presented a certain image, and in the subsequent period that image has proved to be true.

. . . you should really make up your mind . . .

The first of the top three issues is thinking through thoroughly what you really want for yourself and your associates. Secondly, I think, a key issue is to decide very definitively whether you really want to sell. The reason I put it that way is that some people flirt with the idea, and talk to people, and then decide they don't want to do it. I think you should really make up your mind. If you are just toying with it, well toy with it by yourself. And, thirdly, you have to think through how important the money is to you, and what is the weighting of the other factors–like strategic versus financial buyer, not moving the company, taking care of the people that are here, versus maximizing the dollars that you are going to get.

□

Lee White sold (in 1986) a manufacturer of equipment used in the laundry and dry cleaning industry. Sales were $45 million. He sold to an investment partnership.

The best advice is, one, you have to have detailed out what you want to do and what your plans are. Then decide how you want to sell it–on your own, or through a third party to get the widest possible distribution to try for the very best price.

You have to have good numbers, so you have to have a close relationship with your accountant, and you have got to have good legal advice so you know exactly what the legal and tax consequences are.

The book went to at least fifty prospective purchasers . . .

We went for wide distribution. We used a third party, a business broker. We put together a selling book, as it is called, with details of the history, all of the current business conditions and financials, and projects out what your future plans are, and then that is widely distributed. There is a whole network of buyers and sellers throughout the country, and with the right person, these can get very wide distribution. For us, that worked very well.

The book went to at least fifty prospective buyers. From that, less than ten were seriously interested, and we received five bids.

Companies that want to keep everything very confidential might prefer to go through an investment banking relationship and select three, four, or five people that they want to present it to first. They really need to decide what they want to do: they might want to try and sell it to someone within their industry, or they might want to maintain confidentiality from their competitors. They need good advice.

In the negotiations you have to be a very patient person. You have to know clearly what your objectives are and try to understand, as best you can, what the aims of the buyer are.

Top issues: if you want to sell and walk away from the business, then price is a prime concern; if you are going to stay with the business and run it, then I think it is compatibility of objectives with the buyer. We, like most people, were concerned about the interests and objectives of management and our employees.

□

Robert Perfetto made electric motors and sold in 1985. Sales were about $20 million. The buyer was a private investment firm.

If it is a positive, upbeat business, then I think you should have good financial statements for a minimum of three years. You should have a good cadre of management personnel. If it is a so-so business, then try to take steps to manage it in a positive way. One example of what not to do is the 73-year-old who sold me my business. He had stayed on about five years too long, zapped the business for its cash, and went on in a ho-hum manner, and drove the company into debt. When he had to sell it he was in no position to bargain—he went through 43 prospective buyers.

. . . the broker represented himself . . .

You have got to look at it from the other guy's point of view. You can't just sit there and be totally isolated. You can say I want cash only, but you just cut your market down perhaps in half.

You need a good business broker. I've been through the brokers who bring in everybody. A good business broker has knowledge of clients who are looking for businesses of a certain type–as opposed to a guy who is trying to put two things together as if he were selling a house. There are people who go in and try to steal a company. A knowledgeable seller will recognize that immediately, and then he starts thinking about what kind of a guy did this broker bring to me. The broker gets tarnished with that brush as well.

You have got to look at it from the other guy's point of view.

The business broker from California did a great job. He touched base, and he patiently waited out three years. He lined people up along the way, telling them that he had a situation that was developing. He represented himself, truly. He did what a good broker should do–bring two interested parties together, and then he stepped out of the loop. We did the rest. He was paid by the buyer.

You cannot just say "Business as usual, come on in and look at my place." You have to prepare and dress it up. You've got to put together a good performance record, because, if they want bank financing, the bank's going to ask for the data. You need a decent history or the bank is not going to help to finance the guy.

Each buyer looked at the company differently. One said, "Let me take you over, and you can earn more than just the purchase price." But that's a big mistake. When you sell to someone else, you give up the right to manage. If they take the business down the tubes, then the benefits they offered off in the future never materialize. You may sell to less than the highest bidder if someone offers a sweetheart futuristic deal. Now you have turned management over to them. They don't do the things that you would do. The things you had in mind for growth don't happen. Now all they have to do is refer to the contract and say, "Well, this didn't happen, therefore. . . ." And it's the end of the story.

Buyers are, with all due respect, bullshittters. I would recommend that you get the price that you need and want–anything on top of it is fine.

My relationship with the buyer was a good one, but some things that were supposed to happen did not. They were associated with some huge public companies, and they kept throwing at me that they had this great depth of management and capability, and these people used products like mine, and it would enhance my market. I said fine. But I got my price first, and, as it turned out, these huge operating companies were managed independently of them. I can't look back and cry, and say I did the wrong thing. I got the number I wanted.

> . . . professionally managing someone else's business with their money . . .

I was managing the company as its president under their aegis, trying to create the cash to pay the debt that they had borrowed. And so there was no money left to do any fancy things. It was not entrepreneurial in the sense that you were your own man and could do your own thing. You were now professionally managing someone else's enterprise with their money. They asked me to manage the company, and they dumped in the debt, and then it was my job to get the debt reduced.

I had taken everything I owned and put it into the business. I grew the business from about $1.8 million in sales to $20 million. As my years advanced, I wanted to get away from all my eggs in one basket. If, for example, a tornado were to rip up my building, I would have been in bad shape. This way I diversified.

> . . . they tried to change the game right in the middle of the negotiations . . .

At one point they tried to change the game right in the middle of the negotiations. They wanted to make the pay-out predicated on performance. That was a no-no, and I said, "Gee thanks, but no thanks," and got up and left. They called me a couple of days later and said it would be an all-cash deal at your price.

I would not rule out leveraged buyers–for one major reason. They give you the money. You don't care where it came from.

□

James Hackney sold two businesses in 1990: both made equipment for trucks, one with sales of $30 million, and the other with sales of $10 million.

In both cases we ended up with indemnification claims that were substantially in excess of anything we had ever anticipated, and we ended up going to arbitration–there was an arbitration clause in the merger agreement. The smaller business became insolvent, and was taken over by a bank, and we are having exactly the same situation with the bank–a successor-in-interest. In both sales our experience is somewhat tempered by having these lingering indemnification claims which we are having to arbitrate because we couldn't come to an amicable agreement.

. . . first advice would be to recommend arbitration over court . . .

I am very happy we had an arbitration clause in the agreements. Having been through arbitration now, and also having had a great many court cases in the course of my years with the company–I have been with the company more or less full time for 33 years–there is no question that arbitration is much the better way to go. My first advice to a seller would be to recommend arbitration over court with regard to disputes and indemnification. It becomes much more cumbersome if you go to court–both in terms of preparation, and in the conduct of the hearing. There is less that attorneys can appeal, and less opportunity to drag the proceedings out. I can see why some attorneys don't like arbitration. From a client's standpoint, it's great.

. . . arbitration . . . quicker, cheaper, and easier . . .

Our attorney made the comment that with these somewhat complex business issues he looked at this panel of three very intelligent arbitrators and thought about the alternative–twelve average John Does, many of them unschooled in business or anything else. He just shuddered to think of the alternative to arbitration. Not only is it quicker, cheaper, and easier, but you get a better decision. To a degree, arbitration can be a proceeding in equity, rather than necessarily in law.

I would give the same advice that we received, though it is not always possible to carry it out–maximize the amount of cash and minimize the amount of notes. Our notes were subordinated to the senior lender of the buyer–and now the buyer is in default with the senior lender. And in our second transaction the buyer is gone–it is in receivership.

The advice would be to get as much cash as possible up front, and minimize the amount left in escrow for lingering indemnification issues. In our experience, and I have compared notes with others who have been through similar experiences, buyers often count on getting that escrow money back through indemnification claims. It seems to be a standard rule of the game.

Learn as much as you can about *buying* a business.

Other advice I would give is to spend time learning the other side. Learn as much as you can about *buying* a business. Learn how the deal is struck by the buyer, how you go about getting equity, and how you go about getting bank financing. Even though our company had acquired several businesses, we had always done it from a corporate standpoint. We used corporate resources. And we were somewhat babes in the wood when it came to the wheeling and dealing that goes on in deal making. We talked with several different groups, all of them were in the deal-making category, financial buyers.

We suffered somewhat by looking at it from our corporate perspective and not like an individual who would go out and package a deal–put together someone else's equity and bank financing to swing the deal. Had we been more knowledgeable in that area, we would have been able to protect ourselves a little better.

And I have some advice for an owner that is working in the company. The owner is often led to believe by the new group that they don't want to make any changes, and that the intention is for him to continue to run the business–and that is almost never true.

The advice to any owner-manager selling is to assume that he'll be gone just as soon as his contract is up.

As soon as the deal is struck the changes start, and the first change is to replace the owner–in decision-making, if not employment. The advice to any owner-manager selling is to assume that he'll be gone just as soon as his contract is up.

> . . . never, ever, subordinate your income to the senior lender . . .

Many of the contracts include covenants not to compete, and the senior lender of the buyer always wants these covenants subordinated. A very important bit of advice is never, ever subordinate your income to the senior lender. It is one thing to subordinate payments on notes that you may take, it is another thing altogether to subordinate your noncompetition or consulting payments. In so many deals there is a default–and the subordinated payments are held up. In fact, it would be relatively easy to arrange a default. There are a lot of fine points that, as we look back, we could have done better.

We came into contact with the buyer through our accountant. We were both clients of a Big Eight accounting firm. We talked with several companies–Dean Witter, Kidder Peabody, Geneva, and others–and were debating entering into an agreement with one of them when our accountant asked permission to give our prospectus to one of their clients. We granted that permission, and we struck a deal with them.

My duties have changed dramatically. Immediately after the sale, the buyers brought in a CEO of their own. He had been a management consultant, and had no experience whatever in general management. For a while it was a problem for them trying to find something for me to do. Eventually I ended up in charge of a new product we were trying to develop–it was about 10% of our overall sales. It was like going back to chief cook and bottle washer. I ended up doing everything–I became a doer rather than a manager of doers. One of my brothers was terminated.

> The frustration is when they repeat our mistakes.

There is a fraternity of folks who have sold businesses. You tend to share your experiences. We find that our experiences are not unique. A lot of other owner-managers have more trouble adjusting to employment by new owners than we have. Usually there is a fairly prompt parting of the ways. My brother and I have adjusted as well as any former owner-managers. It has been frustrating seeing newcomers do things quite differently, sometimes better, sometimes worse. The frustration is when they do it worse, and repeat the mistakes that we made–in spite of our counsel.

you are the one who is really
being sure you're comfortable
derstand how the deal is struck–
ess, the more you'll be able to
'our lawyer.

..Iost recently, in 1994, he sold an electronics service business with revenues of about $20 million to a leveraged buyout firm.

I would tell a friend to search his soul for a very long time before he decided to sell. For many people their whole identity comes from their business, and when they sell they lose their identity. The question a business owner has to ask is "How much do I identify–myself, my life–with this business, and can I live after I have sold it, no longer really having that identity." I think that's an important question an owner needs to ask himself.

If they get past that, if they decide they can sell their first-born child, then they need to think very carefully about how they want to take their company to market.

. . . whole identity comes from their business . . .

I have sold four businesses in the last fifteen years. Each time I have done it differently. You really need to look at the business, and decide the best way to carry that business to market.

The last but one business that I sold–it made electronic motor controls, and had sales of about $5 million–was to a publicly-held British company with sales of about $500 million. They were a very good customer of mine in the U.K.–we sold a lot of product through them. The British company had a similar business in the U.K., but our products were more complementary than they were competitive. I approached them–I put the bug in their ear one time. I said, "Gosh, with the products you have, wouldn't you like to have access to the 2,500 distributors we have in the United States." It had never occurred to them to expand their market in the United States. That set the ball in motion, and they were extremely interested. At that point they began to pursue me quite heavily.

We sold at a fairly high multiple. It ended up being 10–12 times the pretax earnings. We negotiated over the price, and all the contracts, for a year and a half. We closed in 1990.

The first company I sold was to a competitor–I was in the electrical distributor business. I sold to a competitor who wanted to expand into Virginia–he did not have a presence there, and I did. The second company I sold was to the management. The third company I sold was to a public company, and the fourth sale was to a leveraged buyout firm.

A regional investment bank did some analysis for me on my latest business. I had been approached about selling the business a number of times, and I couldn't decide whether I wanted to take it public, and cash out that way, or whether I wanted to sell to an investment group, a competitor, or whatever.

This investment bank offered to do a great deal of research about various strategies and what price I could expect to achieve. They did this gratis in the hope that I would engage them to help me sell the business. They did appraisals four different ways, and the highest price they could foresee was in the low thirties for all the assets in the business. As it turned out, we sold to the leveraged buyout firm for more than that, but we kept most of the assets–we kept the real estate, the cash and some other assets. It was a slam dunk as far as I was concerned. They were buying on a multiple of earnings, and were willing to pay a very high multiple of earnings, and buy very few assets. They basically bought $3 million of assets for $35 million. That persuaded me to sell to this group.

. . . you should be prepared to walk away . . .

In the negotiations, you should be prepared to walk away. Don't sell from a position of weakness: sell from a position of strength. If you are really and truly prepared to walk away, I believe you'll get a much better price. When this deal was going down, I told the negotiator for the buyer, the worst that can happen to me is that I'll keep a company that is making $5 million a year. I really was somewhat indifferent about making the deal with that buyer. I knew I could eventually make a deal with someone, because I had a very valuable asset. So I was prepared to walk. That put me in a much stronger position to negotiate.

I wanted to get rid of the second company I sold, and I was not in a strong position. When you aren't really prepared to walk, it is hard to negotiate from a position of strength.

. . . after three months, turned in my resignation and quit.

My working life has not changed with this buyer, the leveraged buyout group. When I sold to the British company, I agreed to stay with them, and run the business I sold them, and I became a managing director of one of their divisions–with operations in the U.K. I thought that would be a learning experience and a lot of fun. As it turned out, it was not. Even for a $500 million company, it was a huge bureaucracy, a lot of red tape, and it was a nightmare. I was back and forth to England every two or three weeks for meetings that were utterly worthless. Very little was accomplished–there was a whole lot of pomp and circumstance, and very little real work being done in the upper management group. I became very frustrated and, after three months, turned in my resignation and quit. I couldn't stand it.

My deal with the leveraged buyout firm from the very beginning–and you don't really know if what you hope will happen, will really happen–was if they wanted to run the business they could come down here and run it, or I could run the business and they could leave me alone. They said, "You know the business–we want you to run it, and we'll leave you alone." And they have left me alone to run it. I've enjoyed it. I still have a 20% ownership in the company, but really whether I do or don't, it doesn't make any difference, they've been very good to me. They have left me alone. I am actually working more hours and harder for them than I did when I owned it. I guess I feel a greater sense of responsibility to them than I probably felt to myself. I want to make sure that their investment is a good one, and that they come out well with it when we take the company public.

Of the top three issues, number one is that a seller needs to know what life is going to be like after the sale. To me, that is the most important thing, assuming, number two, that you get a fair price and a good contract. One of the other important things to me was that my people be taken care of, and that there be continuity to take care of the employees who had taken care of the business.

□

"John Doe" sold in 1992 a producer of electrical products to an investor group. Sales were about $6 million.

Number one, you have to have a good attorney, and number two, you have to have a good accountant.

I went to several different concerns–my bank, and other people in manufacturing, to come up with what we thought was a fair price for the company. Then I hired a consultant that I know to find a buyer that would be compatible, so that we could keep our employees happy. We had a good group of employees. He found us a group of individuals interested in small companies.

> . . . you have to have a good attorney . . .

What I liked about it was that it was a group of individual investors looking for small companies to make them grow and retain management, and to make no changes. I signed a contract to stay on for three years until we had my son trained to take over the company, and it worked out very well–I am at the end of my third year now.

I spent one year training my son, and then I semi-retired–right now all I am doing is handling sales and engineering, and my son is running our plants. I retained 10% of the equity, and I will pass that on to him.

I did not talk to competitors for the simple reason that I was afraid that if we went to a competitor that they would change our management philosophies.

I just looked for a fair price. I did not try to put a high price on it, and then come down. I sold the company for six and a half times earnings. I did not try to get an auction going.

Maintaining the integrity of the organization that I had built was a top priority for me. Number two was to find somebody compatible to work with–the bottom line being important, but not number one. We all know we have to make a profit. The third priority was to get a fair price for the company.

□

Sam Newington sold control of a British publicly-owned boat-building business in 1995 to an investor. Sales were some $75 million.

You have to have the right advisors. If your advisors prefer to work on larger businesses, you will not get their best efforts. You must know that the deal will get the attention of someone you respect. I got the B-team from a well-known investment bank to help me at first, and then I engaged a firm of accountants to help me–and they were terrible. You have to look at the size of the company you are selling, and then try to identify a smaller outfit with an entrepreneurial leader who would look after you on a personal basis. You should know that you like and respect the individual who is going to deal with the sale, someone who can show some real achievement in similar situations. We were very small beer to the investment bank people, and the others we worked with, the accountants, were just dreadful–they were really bad. They fired off in a shotgun manner all sorts of circulars about the company being for sale–indiscriminate and indiscreet.

You should know that you like and respect the individual who is going to deal with the sale.

We went public, selling 35%, in 1979 when sales were about $8 million. Then in July 1994 I sold half the family holdings, about 29% of the shares, and I think my mistake after that was, when the same person wanted to buy our remaining 29% one year later, I should have held out for quite a lot more. I should have driven a harder bargain for the remaining family shares, which gave him control. Of course, you wonder when you sell for many millions whether you really need more.

I was mesmerized by the fact that I thought I was getting older, the market was getting more difficult, more litigious, and I just felt I wanted to get out of it. I had had enough. I think I let that color my judgment a bit too much.

. . . I had had enough. I think I let that color my judgment a bit too much.

In the negotiations I was much too quick to accept what they offered. We were a public company, but we were very much run as a family company. My wife and I ought to have talked about it a little more thoroughly, and possibly with our elder children, before accepting the second offer.

I appointed my successor, and I think I did it extremely well and got the right chap–but I never realized quite that I would inevitably be completely out of it myself after I handed over. Obviously, he had to take over the reins from the family that had run the business for 25 years.

> . . . when you have sold the business, you are *out.*

Top issues include getting the right price–which implies getting the *timing* right, to get it a year before the peak, especially in a cyclical business like boat-building. And I think you have to make sure you realize that when you have sold the business, you are *out*. You may not like that if you have been running it for 25 years. You may find it quite difficult to adjust to, which I certainly have done.

□

4
Businesses Sold to Employees

Harry Sugarman made comforters, and sold to some key employees in 1992. Sales were $15 million.

I had a business with a distinct shortcoming. While it was a good business, and a very profitable business, it was a one-customer business. It had a lot of risk for an outsider who did not know the customer, and did not know all the circumstances. On the surface, potential buyers looked and drooled, but when they began to examine the make-up of the company, and began to realize that it was indeed a one-customer company, then generally that buyer disappeared into the woodwork.

. . . it was a one-customer business . . .

No ESOP [Employee Stock Ownership Plan] was involved. I wanted to sell the thing cleanly, and they were aware of the entire situation, and knew it better than any outsider would. They knew it was a good situation. I got what I wanted for it. That was the bottom line for me. For them it was a case of going to a bank, and the bank wound up buying the business, really. The employees put very little into it. Most of the money came from the bank.

I went through several years of listening to a lot of proposals, and, when push came to shove, not getting any solid offers. I began to see that as long as this company was going to operate in this manner–and it seemed to continue to grow with the one excellent customer–this was a big problem for a buyer.

The guys who bought the business know the customer well, and it was a good deal for them. It satisfied me completely. I got all my money out of it.

□

David Halpern made specialty chemicals and sold to a key employee in 1993. Sales were about $7 million.

Get a good lawyer. Not just a garden variety neighborhood lawyer, but a lawyer who understands these things. Talk to a tax attorney. Get everything in writing. Be very open in your discussions. Be prepared to give a little, to get a lot. You have got to yield on some things if you expect to get anything back. Above all, don't let it drag on–if it is going to drag on, you want to sell an option so you can get some money, some up-front money, if they bow out.

If you are selling a chemical company you must be prepared for an environmental study.

Be prepared to give a little, to get a lot.

I would get several evaluations by knowledgeable brokers so you have some idea of its value. Usually people have an unrealistic idea of what their business is worth. If you get several opinions you can get a better picture. It was okay selling to an insider, but they know so much that it would be worthwhile to say you want to keep your options open so you could sell it to an outsider, too. That was one of the mistakes I made–I really should have talked to several people.

Have an intermediary for the negotiations. It is too emotional an issue in a small company. It may be different in a big company. You get uptight, and you might aggravate the situation. I had somebody in between.

Top three issues for a seller: one, have a realistic idea of the worth; two, use an intermediary; and, three, have it all in exact writing. If you are in a hurry, price will probably have to be modified. Be aware of tax consequences. Avoid subsequent liabilities. Be sure that everything is in writing so that you do not get a misunderstanding at the end. Everything should be detailed in your written agreement–go over it once, and then go over it three, four, or five times before you say that it is final.

□

Gilbert DeVore was a principal in a business making proprietary lighting and other products for aviation markets. Sales were $4-5 million, and it was sold to an Employee Stock Ownership Plan in 1992.

If you are selling a technical business, bigger than a mom and pop operation, then there is no use working with a business broker. They don't operate on that level. What you need is an investment banker, and these types can do a job. For years we played with these business brokers who said, "Yeah, I can sell your business." Finally we decided if we were going to sell this business we had to turn off all of these types, so we wrote them all a letter, and told them whatever arrangements we had with them were all canceled. Then we contacted a good investment banking company and worked out an arrangement with them, and they did a fine job for us.

. . . you've got to sell it when the market is right . . .

I guess the timing wasn't right–timing is everything. That's the whole secret. If you want to sell a business, you can't sell it when you want to sell it, you've got to sell it when the market's right, when the time is right, because that's how businesses sell. Anyway, we had a very good investment banker and he sent out about 175 letters and he followed up with a brochure, including financial and product information to those responding. Out of that he received a certain number who wanted to visit. Those that visited were all impressed and very interested, but, when the chips were down, they . . . well, maybe the price was too high, I don't know. . . .

We had set a price so that my partner and I could each realize a certain amount of money. This price was higher than later turned up in the appraisal. On the other hand, we sold it to the employees in an ESOP for much less than the appraisal–because the ESOP regulations permit the seller to avoid capital gains taxes. The employees were delighted because they don't put out a penny. The company pays for everything–it paid for a company to manage the ESOP, do all the paperwork, etc. . . . it pays for the yearly appraisal, and the employees simply get stock. That worked out very well.

. . . the ESOP regulations permit the seller to avoid capital gains taxes.

You have to find somebody that wants a business like yours, or who can mesh it with something they have. Ours was not that kind of a business–it took a lot of development work. That's why we turned to the ESOP. Buyers want projections for three or five years. We had three beautiful years. We projected five years. The first of the projected years was fine. The second projected year we ran into a recession. Obviously, it was not our fault. It happens to everybody. It happens to Ford, GM, Chrysler–to everybody. If things go bad, and there is a recession, the customer base doesn't buy, especially when the products you are selling aren't absolutely necessary items.

We based the ESOP price on what we thought the company could afford. The ESOP had to have at least 30% of the stock, and I being the older partner sold 60% of my shares–and I did not have to pay any capital gains taxes on that, and that is why we set the price lower.

The rules of the ESOP, however, are somewhat limiting.

The rules of the ESOP, however, are somewhat limiting in how you can invest the proceeds. You can only invest in corporate bonds and corporate stocks–no mutual funds, no municipals, no treasuries, none of that. They give you one year to do it, and then the worst part about it is if you invest in a stock and that company goes to pot, you not only lose what you invested in the stock–if you make a change, you immediately trigger capital gains taxes. You cannot buy and sell stocks. You have to pick ones that you are going to live with. That is the most stringent requirement. So if you invested $10,000 in the XYZ Company, and the stock goes down to $5,000, and you would like to sell and buy something else, you trigger the capital gains taxes on the original $10,000 you invested (which came from the sale of the business).

An ESOP is an excellent way for old-time management to get out of a private company and provide something for their loyal employees, and the only thing you have to do is to make sure that they have continuity of management. The employees own the company, but they are stockholders. They do not run the company. My younger associate still owns 50% of the company, and I still own 20% of the shares.

In general buyers like to try to steal a business. Whatever price you set, they knock it down. We had one offer at the price we wanted. But the fellow wanted to move the business. And he wanted us to find out which of the employees would move before he made a commitment. Of course this was unacceptable and we turned it down out of hand. Further, it would not have been fair to our employees who had been very loyal and who depended on us for their livelihood.

So an ESOP is an excellent way to go. It protects loyal employees and continues the business as usual. In our case it worked out fine because my associate was 11 years younger than me, and our Director of Marketing–who was next in line–was about 50 years of age. The ESOP appears to have worked out very well for us.

□

5

Businesses Sold to Foreign Companies

Harris Hollin sold a pharmaceutical company in 1981 to a privately owned German pharmaceutical company. Sales were about $25 million.

> If I wanted to sell a business, I would have to stop and think for whom would the business have the most attraction. And, what kind of person could help me find the company or persons to whom my business would be most attractive–and that is usually a finder. You need someone who is bright, well connected and honest, and understands what you are trying to do, and can help you achieve that objective. So that's Phase One.
>
> . . . as a foreign buyer they made a less-informed choice . . .
>
> Phase Two is to have a realistic assessment of what the business is worth, and to get an offer that will come as close to that as possible, and not get too hung up on getting precisely what you think it is worth.
>
> One reason I sold was that the price was right. Another reason was that I didn't feel that I had the resources going forward that I thought would have allowed us to come out with the new products to continue the rate of growth we had. I think that has been demonstrated by the

fact that the company that was doing $25 million when I sold it is now doing closer to $250 million, but it is doing it based on products that were put into it by the current owner.

On the other side of the coin, shortly after I sold, generic companies became very, very hot, and there's a possibility that I could have taken the company public at a substantial premium over what I got for it–but that's a possibility, by no means a certainty.

When I look back I have never regretted selling at that price. It gave me freedom–it got me away from a very pressured situation where I had been working incredibly hard, and allowed me an opportunity to do other things with my life. I am not unhappy about having been able to focus on something other than that one particular business with the intensity that I had given it before.

I was supposed to stay with the business permanently . . .

I was supposed to stay with the business permanently–the closing took place in March, and they asked me to leave in December.

From the day after the closing nothing changed. I ran the business just as if it were my own. Then, a couple of months later, they sent someone over from Germany to be the chief operating officer. He had responsibility for everything–and I became an executive dealing with acquisitions and things like that. That was not a problem for me except that he did not know what he was doing, and I tried to tell them that, but they were not too inclined to listen: "What the hell could a dumb American know?"

So that was still okay, but what really made me unhappy with them was when they were trying to borrow some money here. They told me what they wanted, and on what basis, and I went out and was able to put together the financing deal that they asked for. Whereupon they went and gave that deal to a German bank. That really annoyed me, and I told them so. That was the beginning of a very changed attitude on my part towards their business methods. When they wanted me to leave that was fine, too. We negotiated an amicable resolution of the equity interest I still retained, and everything was done above board and in a pleasant, business-like manner.

As a foreign buyer they made a less-informed choice than a domestic buyer. One of the attractions of the company to them was that they were going to use it to introduce a number of their products into this country. When I examined their product list, and checked with some of my people, I told them–before they closed on the deal–that there was no way they were going to be able to sell those products in this country. And again they were absolutely convinced that their scientists knew a hell of a lot more about our regulatory environment that I did. I remember saying to them, "Look, it's your money, but don't say I didn't tell you so." And, needless to say, they were unable to introduce anything from that list into this country.

A number of things worked in my favor in the negotiations. First of all, I had a very clean operation–not only in a sanitary sense, but clean in a business sense. The books and records were in good order. Everything about the operation was first-class. That gave them a higher level of comfort when they started digging, and doing their due diligence.

. . . a very negative climate switched . . .

I remember one sticking point in the negotiations: I was having breakfast with two of their people, and it looked as if the deal would fall out of bed. By this time I was emotionally committed to the deal, so I threw at them the suggestion that I retain a 10% interest in the business, pro rata with the price they were paying for the company. What appeared to be a very negative climate immediately switched to a very positive one, and that saved the deal at that particular time.

The effect was to cut the earnings in half . . .

Another flash point was a problem with the audited financial statements. The deal was made based on financials that were still being audited. It was assumed that $500,000 of profit from a particular transaction would be acceptable to the auditors. The buyer was fully aware of all the details of the transaction, and they had included these earnings in reports to their head office in Germany. The auditors' account executive, formerly a friend of mine, kept telling me for weeks everything was going to be okay. We were in the closing in New York waiting for the final documents. I put the auditor on the speaker phone–and he told me then he could not get the transaction approved. The effect was to cut the earnings in half. I turned to the group and shrugged my shoulders, "What do we do? Do we close or do we walk?" They understood the transaction, and they were emotionally committed to the deal by this time, too. We closed. It was a little dicey there for a moment. They were under some pressure on their side to go ahead. They had made public announcements about this acquisition, and it would have been uncomfortable for them had they not gone ahead.

Don't get too rigid . . .

The important thing in negotiations, I have always found, is not to get too rigid. Try to distinguish between the vital, the desirable, and the unimportant. If you can break things down into those categories in your mind, it's a lot easier on your stomach, and it's a lot easier on the flow of the transaction.

The top three issues for a seller are to make sure he wants to sell, because some people say they do, but they don't. People don't have any other interests and they are scared to death of being without the security blanket that the company represents. So it is important to know what you are going to do with the rest of your life, or what you are going to do with the proceeds, or what you are going to do when you are no longer a big shot in your company. The first thing is to make up your mind that you want to sell.

Secondly, come up with a price range at which you are a seller. I say a price range because to hang yourself up on a specific price is crazy, especially if you are getting a lot of money. If you are selling a company for $50 million or $60 million, what is the difference if you get $58 million for it or $56 million for it. To get aggravated over the difference is crazy. Set a reasonable price, and have some flexibility about it.

. . . don't let their personalities, or idiosyncrasies, or your likes or dislikes of them, deflect you from the accomplishment of the goal . . .

The third thing is to stay focused on the deal. You may be dealing with people who are different than you are, that deal differently than you do, but as long as they are capable of going through with the transaction–which you should have determined before you got this far along–don't let their personalities, or idiosyncrasies, or your likes or dislikes of them, deflect you from the accomplishment of the goal–which is to close a deal. I have seen people get distracted by some personality quirk, or something else that they don't like. It is a question of balance. How important is that particular defect or slight–or your perception of a slight–compared to accomplishing your mission?

It's also important to have a middleman who knows what his role is, and doesn't try to do what isn't his role to do, because that can queer a deal, too.

□

Don Joslyn made pressure-measurement instruments, and sold to a Swiss company in 1989. Sales were $5+ million.

It's like retirement–you should get out early. You should get out–in a well-planned way–before you're really ready. Get out early.

> Have a get-out plan right from the beginning . . .

The timing comes from within, through education. You have to educate yourself. You, as an owner, have to study.

Here's the most important thing I can tell a person getting into a business. "Don't get into a business unless you know how you are going to get out." Unfortunately, most of us entrepreneurs, we get in, and we never even think of that question. Somewhere along the way, you have to deal with that subject. And the earlier you start dealing with it, the better. There are some very good professional and academic programs that can help you do that. How to manage, and manage through generations if you want to do it that way.

That's the way I would say it. Get in and learn–and learn quickly how to get out. Have a get-out plan right from the beginning.

I had the business from 1965 to 1989, and I sold a controlling position to a Swiss company in 1989, and then it was up to me when to get out completely. I had my choice–a price based on future earnings, or a guaranteed price. I certainly would not have done it without the guaranteed price.

I specifically looked for a foreign buyer, one who wanted an anchor company, a keystone company, in the United States–because that makes you a very important part of their organization. I didn't want to be the fifth company, and I did not want to sell to a U.S. company. Six years later I am still running the company.

I started formulating my strategy in 1983 or 1984, and I would say that I began actively looking in 1986. So it took three years from then to the closing in 1989.

In negotiations, you can't be afraid to ask. I contacted them myself–I contacted many people. Top issues for a seller are price, terms, and your future in the situation.

□

Frank Hubbard sold a printing company to a British public company in the late 1980's. The business had revenues of about $40 million.

Picking the time is all-important. Timing is everything. We were very fortunate to be in the market when we were doing better than ever–everything was going well. When you have a business like that, people will come and look at your business and listen to what you have to say. Companies that do not pick the right time have difficulty finding a buyer. There were a number of things in our favor. The dollar exchange rate made it attractive for foreign companies to make offers–and we had some pretty nice offers from U.S. companies.

. . . timing is everything . . .

The English company came up with the right price–and they seemed like nice people. They had another printing business in this country, and that worked out well for them–but they did not know much about our business.

We had a lot of negotiations. The best advice I could give anybody about selling their company is that they better have their books straight. Because the process that you go through when the buyer brings in accountants and attorneys is unbelievable. The accountants were in our plant for at least two months. They followed every paper trail from the day we started business, through every board of directors' meeting, every sale of equipment, every land purchase–you name it, they went through it.

We had established the price, and we had even established the time. It looked like it was going to take four months to put it all together. And I mean it was just brutal–you could not imagine. Our people would say, "Why do they keep asking the same questions over and over and over." They would ask the same question to half a dozen different people, and then they would send somebody new in to ask the same questions. It was check, and double-check. And then at the time when we thought everything was finished, that the due diligence was over, then the attorneys came in. And the attorneys started all over again. They looked at it all from a legal standpoint, but the scrutiny of the paper trail was still incredible.

. . . if a company really wants to find something, they can . . .

If someone wants to sell his business, he better have a good paper trail. He had better have straight books because, I guarantee you, if a company really wants to find something, they can.

I stayed on for three years. My working life was not a lot different, but you had to check with them on everything. They brought in a financial guy who was kind of a liaison between our company and theirs. That was a difficult thing because he really didn't know much about the business–but other than that it went fairly well.

The economy did not hold up well during this period, so the earnings weren't what they were when we sold. In fact, the earnings were never as good again as they were when we sold. The timing of the sale was at the pinnacle of our success.

This did affect the relationships. It's like, "How come you are not doing as well as before? You said you were going to do this, etc." It did make it difficult. And this probably led me to ask, "Do I really need this?" I was in the printing business for 39 years. I got to a point where I did not even want to look at another printed sheet.

We had to pay a price for doing it, but we got a very good price . . .

I would say the negotiations for a business this size are always tough. We had a lot of people through the years that wanted to come in and talk to us or to make an offer for our company. I was always very leery about that because you do not know who these people are, and they want a lot of information about your business.

One thing worked for us–it may not work for everybody. We had someone looking over the market for a prospective buyer, as opposed to a buyer coming in and talking to us without any background on who he was. We had to pay a price for it, but we got a very good price, so they brought the right people to the table.

A young fellow called and said he had found buyers for a number of printers. He said, "I have heard a lot about your company, and I am trying to specialize in printing, and I think I could bring some good buyers to the table." That was a different approach from anything I had heard before. He was more focused. That meant a lot. So we talked to him about who he would bring in, how he would go about it, and that whole thing. And we gave him our thoughts.

We were not inclined to go with a leveraged buyout, especially one that required us to leave a lot on the table–we would still be very much involved, but someone else would own it. We had some very nice leveraged buyout offers–almost as good as the cash offer, and we would have had stock in the new company. But after everything was laid out on the table, you had to wonder if this structure would really work–and I doubted it.

. . . they were setting their sights a little bit low . . .

I got a couple of valuations of our company. The fellow who was going to sell our company gave us his ideas about price. He thought the company would be worth somewhere in the low to mid-twenties. I had two other people appraise the company. One of them thought we could sell the company for $30-35 million, and another guy said we could perhaps sell it for as much as $40 million.

I went back to our broker and said he was setting his sights a little bit low. I said we would not even consider a sale below $30 million. As it turned out, we got $35 million. And it was through a lot of hard negotiations. We had a pretty good idea of what it was worth: part of the company was owned by an ESOP and we had appraisals for that every year. The year of the sale our company's results jumped dramatically, and that is why it was difficult to determine what the price should have been.

We were an absolutely clean company. They found absolutely nothing wrong with our company. There were no clouds hanging over us. We had had an IRS audit a few years earlier, and they found nothing wrong. Those things really helped. It gave the buyer an awful lot of comfort—and even so it was amazing how much they checked up on us.

It sure makes sense to pick the right time, to know what your company is worth, and to have clean paper trails.

□

Robert Jackson sold a biochemical business to a Japanese company in 1987. Sales were $5+ million.

The secret probably is don't wait until you either need to or want to. Always keep your eyes open. Don't rush into it at the last minute: that's when you make mistakes.

Look for a buyer that's compatible with keeping the business together, if that is the seller's goal, and he wants to stay with it. On the other hand, if it is a purely economic goal, anyone with enough money is okay.

. . . don't wait until you either need to or want to . . .

I sold a controlling interest in my company to a huge Japanese company, one with 107 subsidiaries. We were able to develop a pretty good partnership based, mostly, on personal chemistry. The next step, of course, is based on performance. With Japanese companies, you find the relationships to be almost more important than the business, at first. Once those are established, of course, everyone reverts to business as usual.

Pretty much, we were able to assess the relationships before the closing. They don't move very fast so you have quite a lengthy period of time to evaluate the different individuals, as they are evaluating you. If you push to rush something along, to meet some personal time-frame, you will find it probably does not work out very well.

From initial contact in October of 1986, the actual verbalized deal was done in early June 1987, and the signing of the documents was in August 1987. It wasn't much longer than a U.S. company would take.

> I chose the Japanese company because I did not want the company bastardized by American take-over mentality.

They paid less than two very substantial American companies offered. I chose the Japanese company because I did not want the company bastardized by American take-over mentality. In the end, all of us who remained shareholders more than made up the difference. We have been very happy with the relationships, and I am going to be a consultant to them in other businesses after I retire.

They wanted a window into the biotechnology market here. I can highly recommend selling to a Japanese company. The secret is, don't be in a hurry.

> Make sure the goal is common . . .

Make sure the goal is common. Make sure that the individual running the smaller entity has decided what he wants to accomplish. Does he just want money, and out, or does he want additional ability to grow, and a financial partner. Lastly, but maybe most importantly, make damn sure it's with people you want to work with if you are going to stay. If it is, it'll work.

□

Robert Knollenberg made laser-based particle-measuring systems, and sold in 1996 to a British public company. Sales were about $40 million.

I would advocate, first of all, using an M&A firm if there is one that you trust in the area. But I would not have them actually develop the prospectus alone. What I think you need is to have someone internally dedicated to that effort. I was lucky enough to have someone who spent a full year doing that–preparing the prospectus, and going out and visiting buyers. In our case it probably took maybe three-quarters of this person's time. This was a retired president of the company.

> . . . have someone internally dedicated to that effort . . .

We tried to keep the activity isolated from our employees, to keep them unaware of the talks. He visited buyers along with the M&A people. It became apparent to us early in the process that the M&A

people couldn't generate the story as concisely—or perhaps as correctly—as someone who knew the business from the inside.

. . . keep the activity isolated from our employees . . .

Top issues for a seller are, first of all, whether to sell, and, secondly, whether you can sell cleanly and leave. For me, I was interested in going on to another activity. I have another company to run besides this one. Part of the strategy was for me to exit after a transition time.

. . . be on guard against people doing LBO's . . .

In hindsight I would be on guard against people doing LBO's. They can consume lots of time. While everything looks like a hell of a good deal, in the end, I would be very watchful to be sure that that was in fact the case.

Most people are not aware we sold to a foreign company. Probably the only concern would be what does your customer base think about a foreign party owning the company, when they used to be dealing with a domestic company. I can't single out any one customer or event that precipitated this comment but it is something to consider.

□

Leonard DeFrancisci made food machinery, and sold in 1992 to a British public company; sales were about $10 million.

If you have any kind of a reasonable business, you will be approached by brokers from both sides of the fence—some representing buyers, and some wanting to represent you.

. . . I prefer to deal with prospective buyers one at a time . . .

Maybe I'm old fashioned, but I prefer to deal with prospective buyers one at a time, rather than setting up an auction atmosphere. A lot of people say you'll get top dollar the other way, not the way I did it. I would prefer to deal with one at a time—if I exhaust one possibility, then move on to another one. Keep my eyes open, but just do it one at a time.

I would advise a seller to look for people that they trust and feel comfortable with, because chances are that they are going to continue to work for the company–and that is why I did not choose an auction atmosphere. I felt that an auction created more of an adversarial relationship from the start, and that was not comfortable for me. Maybe for someone else that is okay.

I felt I had to be very straightforward and open with the people that were going to buy the business, and make sure that we had a good relationship going forward because I have to work for them for a number of years. And I wanted to make sure that there were no confrontations.

That is more important than maybe a few dollars more . . .

I just felt, "Know who you are dealing with." That is more important than maybe a few dollars more, because it is going to be a long-term relationship.

Management now is easier in some respects, and it's more difficult in other respects. On balance it's roughly the same. There's a lot of stress relieved because the bottom line is not coming out of your pocket, or going into your pocket. You don't have to worry about meeting a payroll–and some catastrophe is going to be someone else's headache. But now you have people to answer to that you never had before, and a lot of accountability and a lot of reporting, so that creates some stress of its own.

Being a professional manager entails certain things whether you are managing for yourself, or for your family, or for somebody else. There is roughly the same sort of application, desire to succeed, and roughly the same amount of stress involved.

I don't think people should approach selling their company and deciding that this is great, now I am going to lie back and take it easy. I don't think that really happens in a lot of cases–unless you are retiring.

The price was a formula based on two tiers. One of them was book value, plus adjustments for fair market value of certain assets, like machinery and equipment. All during the negotiations, and the due diligence period, the book value was growing due to profits and we got credit for all of that. The second tier was for the intellectual value of the business and was in the form of a noncompete agreement paid out over five years.

Top issues in our case included feeling very secure that we were going to get all the money, including the noncompete payments. And we did get it extremely secure.

□

Jack Lane sold about 60% of the equity in his printing and prepress business to a publicly owned Canadian company in 1990. Sales were $25+ million.

The single most important element of a deal, if you are going to continue to be involved with the business, is to make sure of your compatibility with the people. If you have no continuing role, get all your money up front.

. . . the more meetings the better . . .

I judge compatibility intuitively. We purchased a number of small companies, and I made the one sale myself, and each time I tried to have a number of meetings—the more meetings the better, really—to see what the people are like. Preferably, the meetings would be over lunch or dinner.

Someone I knew personally had sold to this Canadian company five years earlier, and he was still with the company. I had ongoing feedback about his situation. Then I personally met his bosses several times before we decided to go ahead.

You have to be very careful about earn-outs because I know a number of people in my industry who sold out around the same time I did to firms that were paying them on earn-outs, and in the end they all realized an awful lot less than they thought they were going to.

□

Steve Silver made computer boards for machine-vision applications, and sold in 1994 to a British public company. Sales were around $15 million.

In an industry where the future can be very uncertain, such as the high-tech business–unless you have a company that can be a clear winner in the initial public offering market–you have to find another path to liquidity if you have outside investors. Selling can be the best approach if you find the right partner.

In our case, there was an obligation to get liquidity for investors as well as a desire for personal liquidity. We had many employees who owned stock or options in the company, and I also wanted them to see some kind of return.

. . . you should not negotiate for yourself.

The ideal suitor was one that would provide the objectives of liquidity as well as allow us to continue running the business as a separate, autonomous company. And those objectives were achieved in our deal.

People in the company have hardly noticed any change. A major benefit resulting from our deal is that we now have the ability to run the business with more of a long-term outlook, versus the month-to-month survival mode required when you are thinly capitalized.

I would recommend that you not negotiate for yourself. You have to live with the buyers afterwards, and it's by definition somewhat confrontational. It is always better to have someone represent you. Typically they will do a better job of negotiating on your behalf, and not be as emotional about it. It definitely improves the possibility of having a good working relationship after the deal is done.

In our case we used an outside financial advisor first to negotiate a short letter of intent containing all of the key points of the deal. That made it much easier to get the legal work done in a short period of time.

□

Scott Brown was president of a carbon products business sold to a British public company in 1995. Sales were close to $40 million. A private U.S. company was the seller, but Scott Brown was at the center of efforts to sell the business.

> The first thing you have to do is find out if there are any synergies out there, and, if there are, target those synergistic buyers. That is where you are going to get the best price.
>
> . . . target those synergistic buyers . . .
>
> The way the seller interfaces with the buyer is critical. It is difficult to sell a business on the telephone. When you get down to finalizing a deal, it is best done in person. Stay in the room until the deal is locked up, and then you shake hands and walk out. Trying to deal via fax machines, and on the telephone, takes out the personalities. Credibility can be questioned. Little things can become big things. And they should be resolved immediately–or they just fester.
>
> Select the right firm to represent the seller. Understand the buyer–understand his motives, and the synergies he is seeking.
>
> You want the management of the business to buy-in and support the deal.

□

PART TWO

Steps in Sequence

6
Homework

Learn

Educate yourself. Be prepared. Unsolicited, a suitor might approach you with an irrationally attractive offer–would you recognize it as such? The sale of a business can require some rapid decisions and an offer is seldom left open for more than a few weeks. Become aware of market dynamics now to be ready to make prompt and sound decisions later. Homework will help you judge a proposal.

Subscribe to the *National Review of Corporate Acquisitions*, a weekly newsletter about acquisitions. It reports completed acquisitions, trends in the market, and the acquisition criteria of some buyers. Published by Tweed Publishing Co., 49 Main Street, Tiburon, CA 94920, telephone (415) 435-2175, it costs $175 for a six-month subscription. Here you will learn who is buying what and, sometimes, why.

Socialize Undercover

You must try to understand buyers, and what they are seeking. Consider joining the Association for Corporate Growth (see page 218, in the Appendix, for details). No one would question your interest in learning more about how to grow by acquisition. This organization has monthly meetings in major cities: members and guests hear presentations about how they can improve their effectiveness in making acquisitions. Several hundred people go to the annual convention, and it is an opportunity to meet many buyers.

Study Reported Acquisitions

Develop a realistic sense of who might be interested in buying your company. Buyers of companies similar to yours offer clues. Try to understand the motivation. Get the annual reports of public companies that have bought businesses similar to yours—they will often state why. If you want to see the financial details of a transaction especially interesting to you, and the buyer is a public company, check to see if the buyer was required to file an 8-K report with the Securities and Exchange Commission (SEC). This is required to report an unusual event—like an acquisition—if the transaction was significant in relation to the size of the buyer.

The specific rules for this report are not worth studying—just call a service company that provides these reports about 60 days after the transaction *closes* (not the announcement in the paper of the *agreement*) and ask if the buying company filed a recent 8-K. Disclosure, one such service company, can be reached at 1-800-638-8241 (5161 River Road, Bethesda, MD 20816). Another service company is Federal Filings, Inc. (an affiliate of Dow Jones Company), and its telephone number is 1-800-487-6166. A typical report costs $10–25. They will ask if you want all the attachments: for an overview you don't need them, but if you want to see the actual document used to buy the business, perhaps even including employment agreements, then you need all the attachments—for a little more money. These reports are available on the Internet from the Edgar database (see page 212 in the Appendix).

> Learn as much as you can about *buying* a business. Learn how the deal is struck by the buyer, how to go about getting equity, and how you go about getting bank financing.
>
> —JAMES HACKNEY, page 82

Even if the public company does not have to file an 8-K report with the SEC for the acquisition that interests you, it will often disclose the price paid for a business in footnotes to its financial statements–in its annual report, or in the quarterly report it files with the SEC, called a 10-Q. The same service companies, Disclosure or Federal Filings, Inc., can provide 10-Q reports.

If three or four of the largest companies in your field are the trendsetters, you could monitor all their public announcements (and have them saved for you to retrieve at your convenience) via the Internet website of the *Wall Street Journal* or an online computer service. Better yet, monitor all press releases that mention your type of product or service–you will pick up many press releases that do not get into the newspapers. CompuServe's electronic clipping service mentioned in the Appendix can do this for you (page 216).

Common Acquisition Criteria

Your business may provide an outstanding living, and good profits besides, but still have no appeal to a large public company. Other buyers exist, but the interests of public companies are a bellwether–and investor groups, for example, like to buy businesses they can later sell to public companies.

> You have to be sure that when a new owner takes over the business it is not wholly dependent on your expertise.
>
> –MICHAEL MINTZ, page 14

Here are some common acquisition criteria:

- Predictable profits, above 12% (pretax) of sales
- Average annual sales growth of 12+%
- Proprietary, or branded, products, or some other competitive advantage
- A significant share of a growing, defined market
- Sales over $20 million

- A diversified customer base
- A good management team

Compromises are made: such businesses are scarce. Businesses are bought every day that do not meet these criteria, but you should understand what leading companies are seeking.

Is your business entirely dependent on you? Could it function without you? Management *depth* adds value.

Alternatives: Go Public

Instead of selling the business, perhaps your company could sell shares to the public. Learn the pros and cons. Underwriters will highlight the benefits, if they think you are a good candidate (and they will find you). The best candidates have a sustainable high growth rate, superior profit margins, and a chief executive with a desire to run the business aggressively for years to come. Disadvantages include getting less money out initially, the pressures of continuous public scrutiny of management decisions, and perhaps poor liquidity. A small business with modest prospects does not get much attention, and the price of the stock may languish, especially if you have one or two bad quarters.

You might overlook one drawback: as a small public company you are *less* attractive as an acquisition target than would be an identical private company. It will make no difference if your business is enormously attractive to a suitor, but if your company is ordinary, buyers may not be willing to incur the greater cost and uncertainty of pursuing a public company.

Timing

Think about timing. It is always a sellers' market for an outstanding business. For an average business timing can be pivotal. The *closing* concentrates the mind of the buyer–trends in sales and earnings at the time of consummation are key.

> . . . there probably never is a good time, an ideal time.
>
> –Jack McChord, page 63

If you wait until you have statements showing an outstanding year, the buyer may be facing a downturn as he contemplates a closing–several months after your peak results. Sellers underestimate how long it takes to conclude a sale. Better than a downturn at closing is to start talks with statements showing mediocre results, but with significant improvements in progress as negotiations proceed. The buyer is looking to the future, and will project the *trend* in sales and earnings for years to come. Catch the wave early.

> If you have the luxury of market timing, I think it is critically important to have the trend line of–hopefully both–revenue and profit to be in a positive slope, rather than a flat slope or negative slope. Buyers have a tendency to be line extenders, and they'll pay you multiples on the extension of what they believe the trend lines are. And, much like trading stocks, I think it's important not to hold on to get the highest tick–once the tick turns down on you, you've essentially lost a lot more than if you'd sold a little bit early, when the momentum was still on the upside.
>
> –Ron Marsilio, page 48

Solicitations

You get letters and calls asking if you want to sell. Learn from them. Separate the letters into A, B, and C categories, and discard the latter. Start with the easy separations–in the unlikely event that the chairman of the board of a *Fortune* 100 company writes, treasure his letter. A misspelled, careless letter describing many clients, obviously from a broker, is worthless. Any letter that states that the writer has "clients," in the plural, who are interested in businesses like yours is signaling that this is a broker who is going to look for a buyer if you respond with interest.

A broker writing and describing the specific interests of one buyer may merit attention. Here homework counts–how credible is it that the described buyer is likely to want to pay a fair price for your business? If an unknown party writes, and it sounds both interesting and credible, you should consider writing back and asking for details. State explicitly in your letter that you are not interested in selling at this time, but you would like the information for future reference. Do not, at this point, send product literature. (It is not confidential, but it can send the wrong message.) A cautious owner would have an attorney write and ask for the information, to discourage the broker from talking to others about your business.

A broker may claim to *represent* a given buyer–this can be misleading. Some buyers enter into agreements with hundreds of brokers, agreeing to pay them if they introduce acquisitions that are consummated. So any one of dozens of brokers could claim to *represent* a particular active buyer–what they mean is that they would be paid by the buyer if talks are initiated and they are fruitful.

Be cautious of calls on this subject. A broker indiscriminately discussing your business with potential buyers could complicate your life. Your hint of interest could start a chain of events out of your control.

Synergy

Think about what your business could do for a larger company. Be realistic. Many entrepreneurs have a meager grasp of the strategies of large public companies. Public companies are, in the main, seeking businesses with proprietary products, with a sustainable competitive advantage, and great growth potential. These businesses are rare–and yours might not be one of them. This does not mean it is unsalable–but it does affect who might buy it. Read business magazines like *Fortune* that discuss the strategies of large companies–and continually assess where your business might fit.

Some owners salivate over what their business could become if only it had the resources (sales force, research, dollars) of a larger company–and this castle in the air is what they think, hope, will be the basis for talks. A buyer looks at what you have today, and pays for that. Prospects are important, but the buyer might not share your dream.

Financial Buyers

A common derisive comment about certain buyers is that they bring only money to the table, they have no special expertise to help the business. Before you dismiss such buyers, learn something about other transactions they have completed, and what has happened to the businesses. Sometimes the most important element these buyers offer is a different attitude to risk: they might quickly commit to some acquisitions to grow your business, and make other investments in the business that you would never have made. Money, combined with a willingness to take risks you avoided, could dramatically improve your business.

Pension funds and other long-term investors provide a major source of buying power for attractive businesses. These institutional funds are typically invested via small firms of professionals. These firms, leveraged buyout groups, operate much as venture capitalists do–they play an active role at the board level in the companies, they get a fee from the institutions for managing the money, and, closest to their hearts, they share in the profits when the businesses are sold. They think about how they will get out, the exit strategy, before they invest–they buy with a view to selling.

Over $100 billion, in equity, has been raised by the various firms. They leverage the equity when they buy businesses, and these funds are enough to buy businesses worth hundreds of billions. It is a huge force in the market, and no seller should ignore it.

Think about what it means to sell to such a group. These are buyers using other people's money–they have fiduciary responsibilities. They have a duty to be careful. This means a strong preference for audited financial statements–not something you can create at will. The most critical element for these buyers, most would say, is management. That has to be more than one person, and you may not be their ideal.

Read about leveraged buyouts, the success stories and the failures. Is your company a good candidate? Would you like a minority equity stake in the new company? Could the company's cash flow adequately cover the interest payments to service debt equal to more than half of the purchase price? How long would it take to repay the principal? Could it be managed to produce more cash flow? How would you feel about layoffs, or reading about the business being sold again a few years later for twice the price you received?

> I would not rule out leveraged buyers—for one major reason. They give you the money. You don't care where it came from.
>
> —Robert Perfetto, page 79

Personal Preferences

What is important to you besides price? Do you want to continue to run the business? Buyers of successful businesses want the option of having management continuity. To realize the best price, you should be ready to continue working for about three years.

> I started trying to judge my own mortality. I realized that no one was going to buy my business unless I was willing to put in some time afterwards—and the longer I waited I still had a working period after the sale. And because of my age I determined that I wanted to have some very good years left to do a lot of the things that I have talked about doing. That was another reason to sell, once my son wasn't interested.
>
> —Harold Blumenkrantz, page 44

What working environment will please you? How important to you is the further development of your business? Your answers will help steer you to a compatible buyer.

7

Prepare

Talks with a suitor must develop momentum towards a closing. The buyer sets the pace. If the seller is not prepared, the process is elongated–and more uncertain.

Delay = Risk

A buyer commits, irrevocably, at the signing of the definitive agreement, or even the closing. Not before. Most sellers underestimate this. Buyers–and those providing financing–are constantly reevaluating the merits of the deal right up until the closing. The seller should avoid prolonging the time from the establishment of the price to the closing. The more time that elapses, the more scope for lawyers and accountants to find items to question, and the greater the risk of troubling events like a downturn in business, loss of a key customer, or other setbacks. They may be part of the usual ebb and flow of business, but now they open the door for renegotiation of the price.

> Above all, don't let it drag on.
>
> –David Halpern, page 92

Financial Statements

The price is inextricably tied to the financial statements. They report old news, but they are the best indicator of future performance, the buyer's prime concern. The buyer puts your statements under a microscope, and asks endless questions about them. You will not know all the answers, but just turning over the buyer to your accountant is not the answer.

Have a professional take you on a guided tour of your financial statements. Understand thoroughly the accounting treatments of any unusual items, especially those you say are non-recurring (the expenses you say should be added back to determine the true profitability).

Buyers like to know gross profit by activity or product line–if you don't have it, can you modify your system to get it?

Quality of Earnings

Not all profits are equal. Aggressive accounting, such as recording profits when there is significant risk that customers will not pay, can lead a buyer to challenge your financial statements. Capitalizing product development costs can be controversial. And extraordinary one-time gains, included in income from operations, can reduce the quality of earnings.

Prepare yourself for a discussion with a buyer of any questionable accounting–and, if your financial statements are conservative, understand why, and be ready to present this effectively to a buyer. Using accelerated rather than straight-line depreciation schedules is conservative, and arguably *understates* profits; likewise for last-in-first-out (LIFO) inventory valuations.

Audited Statements

Absence of audited financial statements causes delays. Without them, the buyer has to investigate enough to be convinced that the statements are fair. This takes time. It means having strangers, the buyer's accountants, in your office for weeks. Everyone knows what's going on. At this time, all you have is a handshake or a letter of intent–explicitly non-binding. The buyer can go away after you've suffered major disruptions if the results of the investigation are unsettling–or someone chooses to say they are.

> You can't just go out and sell it. You have to have some preparation–that includes audited books, a history of profitability, and a history of growth.
>
> –Arthur Bollinger, page 33

If a buyer undertakes this investigation of your *unaudited* statements, or offers to pay for an audit using his accountants, you are somewhat ensnared, and vulnerable to a price reduction. An alternative buyer would have to start the financial investigation from the beginning, delaying the entire process. The first buyer may presume that you are unlikely to want to repeat that disturbance–and that you might take a little less to go ahead, rather than choose the uncertainties of a new suitor.

Audits are expensive, and successful entrepreneurs may not need them–until they are ready to sell. Professional accounting firms *review* (for much less than an audit) financial statements: they are printed on their stationery, in their binders, and they convey more credibility than internally prepared statements. The review might highlight some items for discussion, and may provide valuable education.

> If anyone wants to sell their business, they better have a good paper trail. They had better have straight books because, I guarantee you, if a company really wants to find something they can.
>
> –Frank Hubbard, page 101

Compromise

Buyers know the huge difference between a review and an audit. The best compromise, if you are determined to avoid the expense of an audit, is to have the professional accountants come in and observe an inventory count at or near to the beginning of a fiscal year, and again at the end of the year. You ask for no audit work other than this.

Audits cannot be performed retroactively unless the accountants have observed the two inventory counts. If you have taken this precautionary step, you can expect to be able to get retroactively audited statements when you are ready to sell.

SEC Requirements

The buyer, if a public company, may *need* audited statements for your business to meet SEC requirements. Your accountant can tell you the precise rules–a rough guide is that they may apply if the assets or sales of your business represent more than 15% of those of the buyer. These very circumstances, where your business would be a noticeable increment, can offer a chance for a top price.

Recast Statements

You want to show the buyer how much the business can earn–under new ownership. You "recast" the statements adding back costs you have charged to your profit and loss account that would not continue for a new owner. You have to charge a reasonable salary for yourself–the amount a public company would pay a manager for your type and size of business, and any excess over that can be added back in recast statements. Benefits like pension payments are not necessarily an add-back (unless extraordinarily high). The buyer will provide benefits, and these costs will continue. Other expenses, like relatives on the payroll who do not earn their keep, cars paid for but not used in the business, are also added back in recast numbers. Unusual inventory write-offs are more questionable–better to leave such costs in the statements and have a footnote identifying the amount and some details.

You may not want agents of the Internal Revenue Service to study your recast statements. One of many reasons to be careful about who sees your papers, and a reason to get professional advice about the presentation of such adjustments.

The business is probably being sold based on its earning power–a multiple of earnings. This pricing assumes that all assets required to produce those earnings are included in the package. And for a successful business this price is likely to exceed the asset values by a wide margin. Then there is nothing to be gained from restating the balance sheet.

Recasting is no panacea. Buyers are suspicious of all recasting, and will carefully review all suggested adjustments to the actual statements.

Projections

Buyers want to know what profits they can expect—projections of income statements. Most business owners don't have them, and some insist they are unknowable. If your pitch and price presume growth, you cannot avoid projections. The buyer will create them, if you do not. It takes time—and delay can be the seller's enemy. Buyers want reasonable estimates—a minimum of one year, and up to five years. It is tempting to include gains attributable to the resources of the buyer, but after the projected income statements have been studied, the call will come for projected balance sheets and cash flow statements. They won't overlook the capital requirements. Make reasonable assumptions of sales growth, and let the relationships of gross profit and operating expenses to sales have a credible link to those established in the past. Sellers *rarely* give profit projections the attention they deserve.

Business Plan

Professional managers have business plans. A plan provides a road map to support projections. Here you must present the prospects convincingly. A plan merely catalogs what a shrewd entrepreneur is using instinctively to guide decisions, but you're selling more than instincts. You're selling an enterprise that has continuity, independent of your instincts. Quality of management is a preeminent issue when buyers evaluate a business: if you want to look your best, you'll provide a business plan to the buyer. Computer software (see Appendix, page 220) can greatly ease the preparation of a plan. Your accountant, or consultants, could help you. Like a capital expenditure, this is an investment.

> Put together a strategic plan.
>
> —Jack Byrne, page 56

Elements of a Deal

If you strike a deal, lawyers will create a framework for the transfer of ownership. You might sell the stock of your corporation, you might sell the assets, or your corporation might be merged into another company. The buyer will have a strong voice in the choice of the framework, but you, too, have to understand the varying tax and legal ramifications.

A buyer expects certain contractual guarantees and indemnities–and the higher the price the more that will be asked of you. You will, most commonly, have to sign a contract guaranteeing that the information you've provided to the buyer is accurate, complete, and not misleading. Part of the price might be withheld for about two years in case the buyer should have claims against you. If part of the price is in notes, their payment might be jeopardized by such claims. Skilled legal advice is *crucial*, and you should know where you are going to find this help before you receive an offer. (See Chapter 15, Lawyers.) Interviewing lawyers will teach you about the elements of a deal.

Taxes

When a large public company has a subsidiary for sale, one of its first steps is to assess the tax consequences (federal and state) of selling the stock of the subsidiary versus selling the assets (and liabilities) of the business. The difference can be millions. You need a tax professional to make this determination. Have this analysis undertaken before you talk to potential buyers.

Acquirers like to buy assets (rather than the stock of a corporation). Some acquirers will insist that they always buy assets, in an attempt to limit the undisclosed liabilities that may follow the corporation, and to have the accounting flexibility to write up assets, enabling them to reduce future income taxes by increasing their depreciation. Buying stock is not as unusual, however, as acquirers might suggest: when a public company is acquired, it is a purchase of stock.

Sellers' taxes, on the other hand, are usually less if they sell the stock, rather than the assets, of a corporation. If executives of a company are salivating over your business, and there is a competitive suitor, they may agree to buy stock if that is required to win the deal. Alternatively, a buyer may offer to pay some or all of the incremental taxes a seller faces if the assets are purchased rather than the stock. If you don't know what incremental taxes you face, you can't ask the buyer to pay them. Find out early.

Product Literature

Many top executives like to start their review of a business with product literature–before all other documentation. Can yours be improved? Now would be a good time. Collect examples of superior literature that you pick up in shows and elsewhere so you can learn from others.

Easy to Find?

Are you in Standard & Poor's Register of Corporations? You should be. Then anyone looking for a company like yours will find you. Call them at 212-208-8702 (Standard & Poor's, P.O. Box 992, New York, NY 10275) for information about how to be included.

Give some information to Dun & Bradstreet, too. An accurate description of your business will help people to find you. Make sure that the primary SIC code (for your principal business) is correct, and that the secondary ones are also accurate. If you want to help those conducting acquisition searches, then you should give Dun & Bradstreet a reasonably accurate number for your sales. Call 1-800-234-3867 and ask for a copy of your Dun & Bradstreet report: they will send it to you at no charge, and invite you to make corrections.

Pure Play

A pure play is most attractive to a buyer–that is, $20 million in sales in one appealing business, rather than the same total spread among three activities with varying prospects. If you have some mediocre product lines you should evaluate the effect of selling them–such lines might contribute to overhead expenses, but you might improve your balance sheet ratios and profit margins by getting rid of them. Many deals are rejected because the overall gross margin is too low.

Sell Assets?

A buyer might offer the same price for your business with or without some assets that you could sell off prior to beginning talks. The buyer is setting a price based on earning power–any assets not contributing to earnings could be candidates for sale.

Some buyers believe in an unwritten rule–no changes, such as paying dividends, or selling surplus assets, once the talks have begun: changes made while talks are in progress lead to price adjustments. Consider selling some surplus assets or poor-performing product lines *before* starting the main event.

Look at articles about "asset strippers"–buyers who purchase companies and sell off pieces while retaining the core earning power. The sum of the parts is often worth more than the whole. You can do this yourself rather than present that opportunity to the buyer, but do it before the first meeting with a suitor.

A buyer should not be troubled if the real estate housing the business is owned by you personally, as long as an appropriate economic rent is being charged to the business. If the real estate is owned by the company, consult a tax professional–you might be able to change ownership of the real estate before you talk about selling the business.

Practical

A private fax machine in your office is a useful tool at this time. This will minimize speculation among your employees. Meetings have to be arranged, and questions answered. Offers and other papers will be coming for your review. In some offices, like those of lawyers, confidential faxes are routine–and someone might slip and send a sensitive one (perhaps your employment contract) to your general fax number. A private fax number is prudent.

If you have a computer with a fax/modem, you could use a private fax mailbox offered by Concord Network Services (1-800-232-9269). Your faxes are sent (via call forwarding, or direct) to an 800 number assigned to you, and you can retrieve them with your computer from any location at your convenience.

Management

Are you making optimum use of computers? Buyers will be assessing this, and drawing conclusions about your management. This would be a good time to implement some improvements.

For buyers, and those financing buyers, quality of management is critical. Is there a clear second-in-command? Perhaps you should promote someone, or hire. Having a clearly designated heir apparent is a distinct advantage. An impressive management *team* directly affects the price.

If you sell the business, the buyer may want you *and* one or two key associates to sign employment agreements, with undertakings not to compete. If your associates do not own stock in the business, they might wonder what incentive they have to sign a noncompete agreement. This might give them some leverage you had not anticipated. You may be forced to offer them a special bonus to induce them to sign. One solution would be to enter into (assignable) employment agreements, with noncompete provisions, with them *prior to* beginning any talks about selling the business.

A related concern is the possible loss of key managers while you are trying to sell the business. Public companies sometimes offer key managers in a business to be divested a special bonus payable the day after the closing of the sale. This as an incentive for the person to stay and cope with the uncertainties of having the business on the market. Such bonuses typically would be one or two years' salary.

You have to look at this from a buyer's perspective. You could probably run the business without your key subordinate. The buyer, on the other hand, may assume, based on experience, there's no better than a 50% chance that *you* will stay on–and then keeping the second-in-command is much more important. The route to a premium price could be to offer to your top lieutenant stronger economic incentives than your instincts would suggest.

Do you want to stay on and run the business? Can you adapt to being a manager rather than an owner? It may depend in part on the buyer.

Keep your options open. If the buyer wants you, agree to stay—you can both revisit the issue later, if problems arise. You cannot be forced to work enthusiastically, regardless of the employment agreement.

The characteristics that have made you successful—independence, determination, single-mindedness, egotism, aggressiveness—may not make you ideal for the buyer. Think about it. Buyers want to set the future course, and they want you to give all your energy and enthusiasm to function *as directed*. You may not like it—and they know it.

> I hired Gerry Feldman with the idea that he, number one, could prepare the business, in an appropriate way, to be attractive, and, number two, could represent a part of permanent management that was not an owner or founder. Owners and founders, in general, are probably not suitable employees in an acquired company. My brother and I were not there two years after the closing.
>
> —Michael Mintz, page 14

8

Initiate or React?

Do employees feel betrayed when told a business is for sale? Perhaps. And perhaps it depends on how it is presented–but when to discuss it? Few sellers relish this announcement, and many wait until it is common knowledge through the grapevine. This concern about employee reaction, and the impact on team morale, influences decisions about how to sell. Reacting to an unsolicited overture seems to be less of an act of betrayal than would putting out a For Sale sign. It can also send you unprepared into a complex transaction that will completely alter your business life.

> With a small business, it is not always possible to generate lots of buyers. It is particularly bothersome if your first negotiations fall apart, and if you have in advance spread it out to twenty people. I think you are at a disadvantage going back later to the other nineteen.
>
> –Woody Comstock, page 60

Initiate

Anyone will tell you: get people to bid against each other to get the best price. It sounds good. But is your business so attractive that people, enough of the right people, will step up, on your schedule, to bid for it when summoned? Businesses have many idiosyncrasies, and suitors have to commit time and money before they are ready to make a binding offer. It may be hard to attract serious interest.

Furthermore, if you invite people to bid, you have to provide the appropriate information–and there is little you can leave out. The information is shared liberally to attract as many bidders as possible. It reveals your strengths, weaknesses, and plans. Do you give the data to competitors? They could probably realize economies by combining businesses, and it could be worth more to them than to others–but will they offer a fair price? You want the distribution of the information to be carefully limited, but you lose control of it when it passes through many hands.

Auction

Some sellers I interviewed had hired intermediaries to help them to auction their businesses, and they were delighted with the outcome. The choice depends on your business, and your style. An auction has requirements. An agent (usually) prepares a memorandum describing the business (more on this later), and it is then shown to anywhere from a dozen to over 100 prospective buyers. Those tentatively agreeing to value the business highest are invited to study more detailed information, and three or four are permitted to tour the facilities and meet key managers. Then, if all goes as planned, the remaining few bid against one another.

> A business is not a commodity, and not like a beautiful painting that a lot of people would appreciate and bid for in an auction.
>
> –George Nichols, page 23

In this setting, price is paramount–but think beyond the closing. The best price usually comes when you agree to stay–buyers like the *option* of keeping management continuity (they know they have an unlimited right to pay you off at will). If you go to work every day for three years for the new owners, and they irritate you in a dozen ways, this is pain. Stress exacts a price. Chances are your lifestyle will not be affected by a modest increment in the price—but can you weigh this in the heat of final negotiations, when you are under the substantial influence of professional advisors, none of whom will have to go to work every day for the new owners? Perhaps. The pre-eminence of price, especially in a sale by auction, is so intense that other issues may fall out of focus.

> . . . although the three-year employment contract doesn't sound like an eternity, it is a long time, and I think it is very important that you have somebody you can live with for those years—otherwise, you can be an awfully miserable person. That would certainly be a big issue.
>
> —Harold Blumenkrantz, page 44

An auction can, of course, produce outstanding results. But when the bids are disappointing, or the party with the winning offer is barely known to you, it is problematic. Worst is when the winner of the auction has a change of heart, or price, after the other bidders have left. Employees, customers, and competitors now know what is going on. If you withdraw, you have to rebuild confidences—with employees and customers. Too many people now know too much about your business. Key employees may be distracted, and they, like customers, might defect—especially if, as is common, it is on the market for longer than anticipated. The value of the business might *decline.*

> Probably 95% of competitors that would be interested in your business will come in to learn about your business and not do a deal. You need a company in your industry that has some synergy: for example, they make nuts and you may make bolts. You don't want to bring a competitor in and teach him anything because you will wind up paying a price—he will learn from you, and it will be a cheap marketing study, and then he'll walk away from a deal.
>
> —Bob DuPont, page 9

React

To react well you have to have thought about what it is you really want. If businesses like yours sell for five times the pretax earnings, is this acceptable to you? You could hold out for more, and you might get it–but you might have to wait years. Some buyers offer irrationally high prices–but they are scarce. Your business might fit a suitor's like a glove, or some executive with power might covet it for his own reasons–both chances for a top price. To await such a buyer, however, is an uncertain fate.

Inquiries

Brokers (and some buyers) regularly canvass business owners asking if they would like to sell. Is the interest expressed genuine? How likely is your business to meet the buyer's criteria? Many letters you receive accurately outline the acquisition interests of a legitimate buyer. Active buyers want "deal flow"–they want to review summaries of as many acquisition opportunities as possible. You, on the other hand, want to protect your business, and not to have it offered to those with only casual interest.

Here, to illustrate, is an excerpt from a letter sent to brokers by a leveraged buyout firm: ". . . last year we reviewed 2,100 acquisition opportunities, we visited 120 companies, we made offers for 11 businesses, and we bought two." A firm may be genuinely interested in *looking at* your business, but, saying that, they know that there is a less than one tenth of 1% chance of actually buying it. Keep these numbers in mind. This might affect how you react to their interest–it should.

Ready?

You are, nevertheless, tempted when a credible inquiry crosses your desk, or comes to you via someone you know. You like the sound of the suitor, you think the combination makes sense, and you think this organization would offer a fair price. Someone from the company wants to visit you. You face a decision.

Recognize immediately that to get anywhere in talks you are going to have to provide data. Are the statements recast (see page 124)?

Compromise

You can compromise and discreetly invite interest in your company. Selected buyers, perhaps one at a time, can be made aware that you would entertain an offer. Any ensuing talks appear to have resulted from an unsolicited approach. This need not distract your employees or customers.

You want to learn all you can about the style of the company that seems interested. First impressions can be misleading. Suitors curry favor. The executives who make the deal with you may not be your principal contacts after the closing. The quality of the relationship after the closing will be tied to how close your sales, profits, and cash flow are to the numbers you projected. Would you chafe in this environment? The best way to judge the organization is to spend time with their people–and a quick sale is not conducive to this.

Advisors tell you that the process is time-consuming and distracting. It is. They will offer to shield you from sifting through buyers–but judging among serious qualified suitors is not something to delegate. You must participate. Get to know these people. It is worthwhile to spend time with them, answering their questions and hearing about their plans for the business. Accept any offers to let you talk to other people who've sold to them (don't postpone this–do it as early as possible).

> I judge compatibility intuitively. We purchased a number of small companies, and I made the one sale myself. Each time I tried to have a number of meetings–the more meetings the better, really–to see what the people are like. Preferably, the meetings would be over lunch or dinner.
>
> –JACK LANE, page 108

9
Brokers

Why?

Lovers and statesmen have found go-betweens useful–and you can, too. They come with different labels: intermediaries, investment bankers, financial advisors, merger and acquisition consultants, brokers, finders, and others. I shall call them all brokers.

Indirect communications allow you to initiate contacts that might otherwise be difficult or awkward; they allow you to make tentative proposals; they allow you to mull over positions before responding; and a third party sometimes picks up signals that you miss. Most of all, brokers reach more prospective buyers than you would alone.

On the other hand, you do not need a broker if you know someone who wants to buy your business–as long as you are satisfied that this person or company has the necessary resources, will offer a fair price, and will not change it during negotiations. The pool of likely buyers for your business, however, includes many people and organizations outside your circle of contacts. Many buyers make acquisitions regularly, and make their interests known to brokers. Brokers may offer guidance on price, and offer other suggestions, but their most important function is to introduce you to qualified buyers–in the plural. *You* can then choose among the buyers. Brokers' incentives drive them to take initiatives most people would not undertake on their own.

> Identifying the buyers is one of the biggest jobs. If you can do that on your own, that's fine. If not, obviously, having a broker is an important factor.
>
> –Harold Blumenkrantz, page 44

A Quiet Transaction

A quiet transaction, without declaring the business for sale (and perhaps threatening its value), can be appealing. You like the idea of a deal with someone who knows what you have, its value, its potential–and your stellar reputation. This party may be an acquaintance (he has always said, "Let me know when you are ready to sell"), or someone introduced to you by your lawyer, banker, or brother-in-law. You meet for lunch. The suitor showers you with compliments, and the demeanor and conversation convey *class*. You are impressed. You would like to be associated with such people. The appeal of a quiet transaction grows on you. It would be civil.

Wait. The suave appearance and smooth social graces may conceal a larcenous intent. A quiet transaction means, to a buyer, no competitors. Nothing inhibits a buyer from taking advantage of you better than an alternative suitor. Do you want to give a buyer the advantage of dealing with you without competition? Keep in mind that the buyer is only bound when a contract is signed, months away. When a seller deals exclusively with one buyer, the seller is *more* committed than the buyer.

> I missed getting a much broader number of people interested in the business, and a more competitive picture. There were probably people who would have been interested in the business that I never contacted. I probably sold to the wrong company.
>
> –Jim Anthony, page 29

Broker Paid by Buyer

It sounds good: the broker is to be paid by the buyer. The buyer sounds attractive. You provide some information, and wait. A few weeks go by, and you hear that the buyer is not interested. Now the same broker has another prospective buyer to suggest, another company willing to pay the broker's fee. Why would these buyers be willing to pay such fees? It is because they want to review as many acquisition opportunities as possible. The broker's fee adds 2% to a $10 million deal, and valuations are not so precise that this makes a pivotal difference. The problem, for you, is that the broker must heed the buyer: the party paying the broker wants to keep the price *down*, exactly the opposite of your goal.

You take comfort, however, in the knowledge that the broker does not control the price. But a prime benefit of a broker is to create a competitive atmosphere for your suitors. When the buyer is paying the broker, there is less competition. This suits the buyer. A broker for a seller is always looking over a buyer's shoulder to seek a more appealing suitor. Not so the broker paid by the buyer. Some buyers require fee agreements that preclude the broker from introducing an alternative buyer for a specified time–competition is the last thing a buyer wants. Buyer-paid brokers do initiate many transactions, but they do not share your goals.

> You have to live with the buyers afterwards, and it's by definition somewhat confrontational. It is always better to have someone represent you.
>
> –Steve Silver, page 109

So how much do these buyers pay brokers? Nine out of ten buyers agree (for transactions up to $50 million) to the formula 5% of the first $1 million of the price, 4% of the second million, 3% of the third million, 2% of the fourth million, and 1% of the fifth million, and any balance (this is $150,000 for a $5 million transaction, and 1% of the balance). This is called the Lehman Formula. Variations occur. Some aggressive leveraged buyout firms offer a $50,000 bonus, on top of the Lehman Formula, to encourage brokers to come to them first–

and usually this increment is conditional on the broker not showing the opportunity to anyone else for 60 days (broker fees are cheaper than price increases). For a $25 million transaction the "Lehman" fee is $350,000, 1.4% of the total. Clearly, this has a minimal effect on the economics of the acquisition.

Many sellers choose to avoid a financial commitment to a broker and rely on buyer-paid brokers to introduce them to a series of suitors. This restricts their universe of buyers. Almost all leveraged buyout firms agree to pay brokers for initiating acquisitions. So buyer-paid brokers can introduce a wide variety of such suitors. The large public companies are different: with notable exceptions, most do not pay brokers when they buy. They are presented with plenty of acquisition opportunities by agents for sellers, and they approach some target companies on their own. An aggressive manager in a public company may not worry about a 1–2% increment in the cost of an acquisition, but he runs into procedural barriers: company policy may preclude buyer-paid broker fees. Rely on buyer-paid brokers and you miss some important segments of the market.

. . . get a broker. I have sold two businesses through brokers. The advantages of selling through a broker are that you have a much broader market, and you get a more valid evaluation of what the business is worth because of the broker's exposure to many buyers.

Having the buffer of a partial negotiator, the broker, who wants to make the deal, is very, very important because he can feel out the emotional climate, and can have a more realistic evaluation of the emotional climate. He can make a more realistic evaluation of the feelings of both buyer and seller. "Doctor, don't treat yourself." "Lawyer, don't represent yourself." You want some unemotional involvement. The broker can be a kind of referee.

–Marvin Levine, page 61

Broker Paid by Seller

If you agree to pay the broker, you face some decisions.

- Is it to be *exclusive*? Is the broker to be paid regardless of the source of the buyer? If it is exclusive, you pay the fee even if the ultimate buyer is your cousin, or anyone else you might find on your own. One variation is to have it exclusive except for a small number of identified companies or people.
- What about a monthly retainer? Wall Street firms insist on this, and an exclusive arrangement. It could be $10,000-20,000 per month, and it is not refundable (but it is usually deductible from the sum payable at closing, sometimes called the success fee). You will be told it is to show a commitment on your part, to establish that you are seriously interested in selling.
- Are you sure you want to sell, or does it depend on what kind of deal you can make? Are you comfortable striking the best deal you can in 3-6 months, or do you want to allow more time?
- What are your views on an Offering Memorandum? Do you want to have one prepared? Some brokers will suggest a charge for the preparation of this document, perhaps in lieu of a monthly retainer.

A non-exclusive agreement should state that no fee is payable if the transaction is consummated more than two years after the introduction, or if you have had talks with this party on this subject in the preceding two years.

> A facilitator, like a broker, is very important. Someone who can listen to both sides. He can get the buyer's negative points, and positive points. The buyer might be more open in talks with the facilitator than in talks with the seller.
>
> A broker can research the market. He can ask if a buyer would be interested in a type of company without revealing the name—something the principal cannot do.
>
> —Jim Cullen, page 26

Why Sellers Use Brokers

A broker provides access to buyers. You choose among the buyers, but you need the introductions. Unlike you, a broker can call an habitual buyer and describe a business for sale, without identifying it. Likes and dislikes of buyers vary over time. Their workload changes. They practice triage–work on the best, or largest, opportunities first. Timing counts: a description might produce a negative response one day (when they are concentrating on something else), and a positive one a month later (after the collapse of the other option).

The highest price can come when a business fits with one the buyer already owns; habitual buyers make brokers aware of what they are buying, and the add-ons they are seeking.

> I think my problem was fear of having my customers and my competitors hear that we were for sale. . . . In hindsight, I would probably have done better to have gotten the word out into the market, . . . and that could have made a big difference in the ultimate price. . . .
>
> I had a good friend in the merger and acquisition game advising me on the sidelines, and that was exactly his advice. I was just afraid to take it. He was right, and I regret that I did not listen to him. . . .
>
> –Robert Girvin, page 21

Don't delegate the screening of buyers entirely to a broker. This is your chance to evaluate buyers as they evaluate your business. You want a chance to judge nuances of style and look for early warnings of troubles that might follow the closing.

Brokers can seek concessions in the negotiations over issues you might be reluctant to fight for yourself. And staying one step removed from a confrontation allows you to avoid fraying relationships, and gives you time to mull over a compromise solution. Lawyers often play this role, but they are constrained: it is unethical for a lawyer to call the *client* on the other side; your lawyer must communicate with the buyer's *lawyer.* But a broker can call the buyer's vice president for acquisitions, or whoever is handling the deal, and try to resolve an issue informally.

> . . . they really create a competitive environment which I think in the end results in a higher price–and they pay for themselves.
>
> –Ken Poorman, page 43

If a seller has a broker, the *atmosphere* is different–a buyer assumes other suitors are being encouraged to make offers, and the threat of competition influences any price proposal.

How to Begin

If your business is attractive enough to permit a successful auction, and you are comfortable with the process, this should result in the highest price. If an auction is not for you, consider the following:

- A broker can introduce buyers unknown to you. A buyer-paid broker will not seek to optimize your position.
- Broad distribution of an Offering Memorandum is not appealing. Too many people get too much information about the business.
- Some aspects of a quiet transaction are attractive. Employee morale is important, and any negative impact on the business is *deadly*. A broker can approach a small number of qualified buyers.
- A go-between can listen to both sides, and insulate outbursts. You have to work with the buyer in the future.
- A monthly retainer creates a pressure to close within a limited time–and you may have reservations about the best buyer found in the first six months.
- You can put your toe in the water. Find a broker to your liking. No exclusive. No retainer. No Offering Memorandum; provide a business plan to chosen suitors. An agreement to pay if a sale is consummated. How much? Probably the Lehman Formula. Some like to switch the incentives–make the percentages increase as the price

goes up. You probably pay more this way. It may not make much difference–the prime incentive is to produce a closing.

- You want to avoid being shopworn. The prime route is unrealistic expectations–about who might buy the business, and your price. And letting several brokers look for buyers might result in targeted buyers being approached about your business more than once, leading to the "shopped" label. Give one an *effective* exclusive for a while–nothing in writing guaranteeing an exclusive, but a conscious decision to let one broker work on your behalf for a period, and to assess the results. Let this person know the leash is short, the future uncertain.
- Steps taken here are reversible at will.

This is your show. Make the broker sign a confidentiality agreement. Let the broker persuade you of the merits of each suitor. Without your cooperation at each step, the broker cannot function. This is your ultimate weapon. Require your approval before confidential information about your company is given to anyone–discrimination is required to choose who receives the data: make those judgments *yourself*.

> You have to look at the size of the company you are selling, and then try to identify a smaller outfit with an entrepreneurial leader who would look after you on a personal basis.
>
> –Sam Newington, page 89

10
How to Sell Your Story

Guard Sensitive Information

Making it easy for the buyer is not your only concern. Some sellers do well by leaving a few hurdles for buyers. If all the information is readily available, it inevitably goes to some people who are only casually interested. If you have an attractive business, and don't want to reveal too much in early talks–before you know the character and motives of a suitor–you can dribble information out in stages.

Start with *strategic* buyers, those looking for a business fit. Not only can these buyers pay more than others, they can make an initial determination of their interest by looking at product literature. Financial statements can be summarized orally for them. Some sellers might question how much more information they want to provide before meeting someone.

If, however, the business is to be sold in an auction, you need an Offering Memorandum–called a "book." This lists reasons why the business is attractive, it provides some history, a description of the industry, products, facilities, management, competition, and the outlook. It analyzes sales by product line, and usually reveals profit margins by product category. Schedules of financial details are included. It may tell too much. You don't mind giving that to someone who buys the business, but what about all the other people who see it?

Some businesses are in demand, and sell quickly. Others are mundane, and it takes months to find a buyer. The Offering Memorandum has data that reveal when it was written. It can be rewritten, but in practice that seldom happens. Buyers can see how long the business has been on the market by the age of the Offering Memorandum.

Business Plan versus Offering Memorandum

A business plan can substitute for an Offering Memorandum. Companies raise venture capital by showing potential investors their business plan. Readers expect a business plan to be prepared by management; readers expect Offering Memoranda to be written by agents. A business plan is especially appropriate for someone unwilling to be openly for sale. An Offering Memorandum suggests you expect to sell the business within the next several months. A business plan sends no such message, and it does not have to be prepared in secret. If a buyer picks up a business plan six months after it was written, it has no special significance. This could be supplemented by a letter with some key facts not in the plan, such as details of ownership, background of management personnel, reasons why the business is an attractive investment, and some of the history.

Confidentiality Agreements

Confidentiality agreements are usual before information is provided. (Consider whether you want one signed before your name is revealed.) The protection provided is not watertight, but large organizations want to avoid litigation. You probably want the confidentiality agreement to provide that, if no business combination occurs, the suitor will not offer a job to any of your employees for a period of two years. Employees in large corporations are sometimes looking for businesses to buy themselves, while masquerading as having interest on behalf of their companies. Asking such people to sign a confidentiality agreement on behalf of their employer usually requires review by colleagues, thus discouraging deception.

Be alert even after a confidentiality agreement has been signed. Get a sense of the motives of the people, the price they would pay, and the odds of completing a transaction with this party before revealing your secrets.

Unions

For some buyers this is a threshold issue. If you have a union, make it known early to avoid wasting time with suitors who would not close: a buyer with no unions might be unwilling to change this status.

Meetings

Meetings–when, where, and who–are part of your negotiating position. Buyer usually comes to seller, to see the business. Buyers want to know and see everything, but it may not suit you to acquiesce immediately to all their requests. Protecting your business *must take precedence over* accommodating a suitor.

> We tried to keep the activity isolated . . . to keep employees unaware of the talks.
>
> –Robert Knollenberg, page 105

If you have proprietary technology or systems, or very sensitive employees, you may not want anyone touring your facility until you have a strong sense of where the talks might lead. A cautious seller will suggest a first meeting away from the business. You could meet a suitor for breakfast or lunch at some mutually convenient spot. If the buyer is making a special trip of hundreds or thousands of miles, you can hardly suggest you limit your talks to a nearby coffee shop. For such people you may agree to meet at an industry convention or in some major city where you both have other business. Or you could visit the buyer.

If your lawyer is your confidant, you might consider having the first meeting at his office, but many of these exploratory meetings are fruitless, and it will be expensive if the lawyer is in at the outset for each suitor. And the atmosphere of a lawyer's office is not conducive to quick rapport.

Buyers like to meet the management team, not just the owner. Resist the urge–often quite strong–to please the buyer. Don't introduce buyers to your key employees until you feel confident that a deal is likely to be made.

> What I think you need is to have someone internally dedicated to that effort. I was lucky enough to have someone who spent a full year doing that–preparing the prospectus, and going out and visiting buyers. In our case it probably took maybe three-quarters of this person's time. This was a retired president of the company.
>
> –Robert Knollenberg, page 105

Qualified Buyer

Visitors should be qualified in advance–you should be given background information (an annual report or other literature), and it should be clear that they have the necessary resources or a demonstrated record of being able to finance acquisitions. Buyers can be told the asking price in advance of a meeting, but this does not inhibit them from offering less, perhaps much less, after time-consuming talks. Buyers, too, want to avoid spending money on fruitless tasks, so they'll be alert as to how many others are interested in the business–a reason to make them aware at the outset that you are talking to other (unnamed) prospective buyers.

Many buyers plan to use other people's money. Don't be reticent. Ask about the funding. Ask how much equity the buyer would invest, and how much they plan to borrow. Where is the equity coming from? Does the buyer plan to produce a document describing your business and then send it to various financing sources? Understand the process–bankers may be coming to ask questions about your business, and you might be the principal salesman for the financing. Know this at the outset. Don't be surprised. Ask about other transactions this buyer has concluded. Learn how prior acquisitions were financed.

> I really sold the business to his creditors.
>
> –"John Doe," page 30

Visit Buyer

At the first meeting buyers are trying to find out if the owner will stay and manage the business–and they are judging how well the relationship might work. You are making similar assessments, but yours are more difficult. The first visitor is unlikely to be your main contact if you sell to this organization. If you are invited to visit the buyer's office, accept. Here you will meet more senior people, who do not go on exploratory trips. You will get a better understanding of the organization, and why they are interested in your business–and an initial grasp of how committed they are to the purchase.

Buyer's Focus

Buyers will concentrate on certain elements of your business. And this is where you must present facts and judgments in the best possible light.

- Historical financial statements are the foundation for presenting the earning power. If yours understate the earnings, carefully tabulate and explain the adjustments to show what the earnings would be under different ownership.
- Buyers will have visceral views of the characteristics–trends, size, growth, threats–of your industry. Since they may well be wrong, you must present, on paper (in your business plan), your view of the potential, *and the basis for your position.*
- Your competitive advantage–your strengths versus your competitors'–will be scrutinized. Don't neglect to make your case.
- If you leave gaps in the story, be assured that the buyer will fill them. Present a complete picture to control first impressions.

> . . . you have to find a way to make the perception of your strengths stronger than they are . . .
>
> –Martin Gould, page 27

11
Leveraged Buyouts

Most leveraged buyout (LBO) firms get their money for investments from pension funds, universities, insurance companies, and other institutions. The firms earn a fee for managing the money, and a *carried interest*, an equity participation in purchased businesses on favorable terms. The prime motivation of most of their executives is the share of the profits they earn when they sell a business. They are called financial buyers because their interests are *generic*–they like almost any business if the numbers are appealing.

Qualify?

Debt-free businesses are most attractive to LBO's. Any interest-bearing debt in your company is subtracted from a price they would otherwise offer (see next chapter). The cash flow from your business must be sufficient to service the debt.

An LBO firm evaluates businesses like anyone else–looking at earnings consistency, margins, management, and prospects. In theory, growth is not a key element for an LBO (the textbook case maximizes free cash flow to pay down debt, with minimal funding required for expansion), but in practice every buyer likes growth–better for going public, or for "flipping" the business (a quick resale).

Pricing

An LBO firm generally pays no more than about six times the earnings before interest and taxes–perhaps up to eight times for a truly superior business in a very buoyant business climate. For transactions of $30 million or less, many LBO firms aim to pay about five times the earnings before interest and taxes–for businesses with no interest-bearing debt.

You might get more if your business is a synergistic addition to one already owned by an LBO firm. Look for signs of firms buying several businesses in the same field. Such consolidations are efforts to buy enough businesses to make the total large enough to go public or to sell to a big public company. By consolidating, these firms hope to effect economies and improve margins. They may pay a top price if your business would fit such a plan.

> I think it is important to find a synergistic buyer. They are clearly able and willing to pay more. They are looking to the future. A lot of times financial buyers buy the past, but a synergistic buyer can create a new and brighter future. So he'll pay more, and you can demand more, because it's worth more to him.
>
> –JONATHAN DILL, page 50

Debt

The buyer looks at your assets and cash flow and estimates how much a bank would lend, secured only by the resources of your business. Asset-based lenders usually are willing to lend around 85% of Receivables, 50–60% of inventory, and a negotiated proportion of the market value of fixed assets–*if* there is sufficient cash flow to service this debt. Some institutions will lend based on the cash flow of the business. If the debt the business will support is less than half the price, then the interest of the LBO buyer may wane. If it is around 80% of the price, enthusiasm should be evident.

The simplest leveraged acquisitions call for 70-80% of the price in bank financing, and the balance of the price provided by equity from the pool of institutional money managed by the LBO firm.

Lenders look at the *interest coverage*–your annual cash flow from the business must be at least 1.5 times the annual interest on the contemplated debt; some conservative investors, willing to commit more equity, will seek 2.5 times interest coverage.

Before you shake hands on a price, you should see a pro forma balance sheet of your business after the closing, one that includes all the acquisition financing. Where do obligations to you stand? Is a note to you subordinated to bank debt? Are payments for your noncompete agreement subordinated, and to whom?

Mezzanine Money

Mezzanine money–financing that has some elements of debt and equity–often fills a gap required to meet the price. This might be subordinated debt with attached warrants or convertible preferred stock paying a dividend, so that it offers the holder a current yield, plus some opportunity for a capital gain if the company is sold at a profit. This is attractive to some institutional investors.

A $20 million purchase might have $13 million of bank or other senior debt, $4 million of mezzanine money, and $3 million of equity. Some firms offer investors a "strip"–an institution might be asked to purchase a combination of senior debt, a mezzanine position, and some equity. Mezzanine money is usually no more than about 30% of the total transaction. Banks and other senior lenders look upon mezzanine money as akin to equity, and hence its key role in allowing a buyer to offer more for a business.

Mezzanine money is scarce for small transactions. Most commonly it is at least $5 million, and is therefore rarely present in transactions of $15 million or less. And you may be asked to fill the gap.

Seller-Financing

Seller-financing are words you do not want to hear. The buyer is asking you to lend money to the new company. Worse, the debt to you is to be subordinated to the bank debt (almost assuredly the case, but seldom made clear to the unsuspecting seller until the last minute).

Seller-financing is most likely to be proposed for deals under $15 million. If the price is $10 million, and the bank is willing to lend $6 million on the assets, you may find the LBO buyer unwilling to put in $4 million of equity. The buyer may ask you to take a note for $2 million of the price. In this example, you would have as much money ($2 million) at risk in the new company as the LBO investor: so you might want to bargain for a share of the upside potential (and, on principle, you want to be sure that you do not have *more* at risk than the buyer).

If the bank does not get paid interest and principal on schedule, any payments to you will likely be frozen. And payments under your noncompete agreement may be similarly stymied. To reflect the risks, some buyers are offering interest rates of around 15% on these notes in 1997, more than double the prevailing rate for top-rated corporate bonds. The track record of the buyer in other deals, and your knowledge of the cycles in your industry, will be your best gauge of the value of the notes.

> You have got to look at it from the other guy's point of view. You can't just sit there and be totally isolated. You can say I want cash only, but you just cut your market down perhaps in half.
>
> —ROBERT PERFETTO, page 79

Interest-Only Note

Mezzanine money typically will have no amortization of principal in the first two years, and you are unlikely to do better for your seller notes. Banks, who can dictate many of the rules, like to see a substantial share—perhaps half—of *their* principal returned before they agree to principal repayments on the seller notes. The buyer will want to repay your principal all at the end of the term in one "balloon" payment. Try to negotiate for principal payments to begin quarterly after two years.

Covenants in Loan Agreement

When an insurance company lends money to a business it requires covenants in the loan agreement. They provide for sanctions if, for example, the net worth is not maintained above a certain level, or if various financial ratios fall outside a negotiated range. If a billion-dollar company provides seller-financing when it divests a business, it will also insist on covenants. So can you. They will not make a bankrupt company solvent, but they may give you some bargaining leverage if the business turns sour. The buyer may have to come to you to seek waivers from some of the covenants: breaching the requirements of the note you hold may make it due and payable immediately; it may trigger an increase in the interest rate; and it could interfere with other financing plans of the new company.

Note Secured by 100% of the Shares

This *sounds* good. The buyer may offer to secure the note with 100% of the stock in the company you plan to sell. You get the company back if there is a default. The catch is that it will not be the same company. If you were to get it back, it would be highly leveraged–with debt it is unable to service. The company would be on its knees.

Capital Pool versus Separate Funding

Some firms do not have pools of funds. They raise money for each deal as it arises. Ask. It can make a difference. You should know if they intend to shop for equity financing. It will take longer and mean more documentation, more visitors to your business (as prospective investors examine the property), and more uncertainty. Investors are not irrevocably committed until the papers are signed–and this occurs after months of disruption of your business.

Those raising money for each deal have to negotiate how much equity they get for their efforts–it is disproportionate to the money they invest because they are compensated for arranging–promoting–the deal. A firm might offer to buy your business for $45 million, but it might be contemplating investing no more than $1 million of its own. You should know the financing plan–the price is not secure if investors unknown to you have to be persuaded of its fairness.

Some firms are investing their own capital–amassed from earlier successful investments. They can be more flexible than those investing institutional money in accordance with prescribed rules.

Business Pays for Itself

When you, as a sophisticated seller, ask to see details of the proposed LBO, you might conclude that the business is being bought with its own money–not an original observation. While it might look as if you could help your nephew to buy it the same way, it is not so. Lenders and investors for buyouts support those who have done it successfully before–people who will change management ruthlessly if the business falters, who will aggressively seek to add value by buying complementary businesses, and who will squeeze cash out of the business in every possible way. And investors want an exit–the sale of the business again.

Employee Stock Ownership Plans

If an ESOP buys your stock it may be an LBO, but not necessarily. A company can make tax-deductible contributions to an ESOP in lieu of to a qualified pension plan. These funds accumulating in the ESOP could gradually buy your shares. An ESOP often will borrow funds based on the assets and cash flow of your company, and use this loan to buy some of your shares.

> An ESOP is an excellent way for old-time management to get out of a private company and provide something for their loyal employees.
>
> –GILBERT DEVORE, page 93

There are special tax advantages for the selling shareholders, the company, and the lenders. Complex rules apply. Houlihan Lokey Howard

& Zukin is a firm that provides advice on ESOP's. Contact them at 1930 Century Park West, Los Angeles, CA 90067 and ask for their booklet on ESOP's.

Approval of the Bank Loan

Approval of the bank loan, a pivotal event, usually comes very late in the process–long after the agreement in principle has been signed, often after a special financial audit, an environmental audit, and the due diligence, by both the buyer and the bank, are essentially over. If the bank decides against the loan, buyer and seller are left high and dry.

Equity in the New Company

The LBO buyer may offer you, or one of your children in the business, equity in the new company. Be sure you understand this. If the purchase price is $10 million, bank debt is $6 million, subordinated debt $2 million, and total equity is $2 million, then the value of, say, 20% is at the outset $400,000 (not 20% of $10 million).

More subtle is an offer to buy 80% of your business for, say, $32 million. You might conclude this is equivalent to a valuation of $40 million for 100%, but when you read the small print (much later than the original offer) you are likely to find that you have 20% in an entirely different company, now highly leveraged–and you have, in effect, provided seller financing to help the buyer restructure the balance sheet. To shine light on the true economics, offer to sell for $40 million, and say that immediately after the sale you are willing to invest in equity in the new company on exactly the same basis as the new investors. In any event, if you invest in the new company, it should be pro rata, on the same economic terms, as the other equity investors.

The value of the leveraged equity in the new company may grow rapidly if the debt is paid off as planned. A subsequent public offering might be a windfall, but it is not without risk. And minority ownership in a private company is a very illiquid asset–for an indefinite time. The majority owners will be making the key decisions, and you'll be virtually powerless. If all goes well, you'll profit when they sell, but when plans fail, acrimony can develop.

> There are so many nuances in the negotiation and sale of the business, and you are just not prepared for it, unless you have done it before.
>
> –Jack Parlog, page 54

Will It Close?

LBO's often founder when the financing plan fails. The conundrum is that you will not know if the plan is sound until several weeks after agreeing on a price–long after you have stopped talking to other suitors. Final approval of financing usually comes shortly before the closing.

People who buy businesses routinely do not, of course, want to waste time on acquisitions that they cannot finance, but they sometimes invest time in deals that are at the margin. After all, the most desirable businesses command high prices, and that drives the financing plan to the edge. Use every opportunity to learn more about the financing plan, and to assess how speculative it might be.

Keep in mind that the 60-90 day due diligence period often gets extended–and that may not be bad. If a buyer has made a good-faith effort to complete the transaction on time, but has run into some unforeseen problems (perhaps discovered an environmental problem), you may want this buyer to persevere beyond the 90 days. Starting again with someone else would set back the timetable–and the same problem might arise. If asked to extend the time for exclusive negotiations, mull it over carefully; it is not a routine step. By now, you know the buyer much better, and the bloom may have wilted. Disappointing as it will be, and difficult to admit to those around you, it may be time to look for a new buyer.

A large corporation, discussing a sale to an LBO buyer, and vigilant about pitfalls, will demand to know the status of the financing. The LBO firm might let them talk on the telephone to people at banks and providers of mezzanine money. Executives at the money sources are likely to be straightforward–and say that the loan is not yet approved, but that it has an excellent chance of approval from what they have seen. You could ask for such reassurance.

Not for You?

Most business owners dislike debt, and therefore do not react favorably to borrowing much of the purchase price based on the assets in the business, yet this category of buyer may be your best opportunity to sell the business. People who run these firms are in business to make acquisitions: that is what they think about when they get to the office every day—unlike operating executives in public companies, who can agonize over fit and risk.

But keep alert. An LBO buyer, proposing to pay all in cash, may say that it isn't your concern how the purchase price is financed. It is, of course, if you value goodwill built up with employees, customers, suppliers, and the community: a buyer unable to meet commitments a year or two after the closing would create anguish.

LBO buyers are an *enormous* factor in the market. In October 1995 the *National Review of Corporate Acquisitions* newsletter reported that buyout groups had increased over the preceding decade from 40 firms managing $7 billion to 214 firms managing $93 billion. This capital, when leveraged with debt financing for each investment, represents well over $200 billion of buying power—are you going to ignore this huge segment of the market?

> We had some very nice leveraged buyout offers—almost as good as the cash offer, and we would have still owned stock in the company. But after everything was laid out on the table, you had to wonder would this structure really work—and I doubted that it would.
>
> —FRANK HUBBARD, page 101

12
Price

Price is not everything. Feeling right, overall, about the sale a year or two later is more important. If you are to continue managing the business, your happiness will depend on much more than the price.

> In our case, the price was the third element.
>
> —Mayer Mitchell, page 32

Factors Beyond Your Control

Interest rates, bank lending policies, stock prices, general business confidence, and trends in your industry are all relevant to how much you can get. Let these factors influence your *timing.*

Folklore

Industry insiders sometimes talk of a rule of thumb in valuing companies in their field—120% of revenues, 100% of revenues, etc. Knowing the industry folklore is useful if you can use it to your benefit in negotiations, but clearly the top line of the income statement is only part of the story. Sophisticated buyers will pay scant attention to these rough-hewn benchmarks: they will scrutinize the potential profits.

Some say financial buyers pay wholesale prices and public companies pay retail. Read on, and draw your own conclusions.

> The most important issue for a seller is timing . . .
>
> —RON MARSILIO, page 48

Projected Profits

A rational buyer determines the upper limit of the price based on the expected future earnings. Your business plan should project future profits with persuasive documentation. (See suggested business plan software in the Appendix, page 220.) If you do not provide projected sales and profits, buyers will create them, and run them endlessly through their own computer models, using different assumptions for interest rates, growth rates, and other variables.

Financial Buyer

A multiple of the pretax earnings or cash flow drives the pricing for LBO or financial buyers. If the company for sale has bank or other interest-bearing debt, a financial buyer will deduct that from the price derived from the multiple of earnings. The multiple will be of the earnings before interest and taxes (EBIT), or the cash flow—the sum of earnings before interest and taxes plus depreciation and any other amortization (EBITDA).

A buyer, willing to use an earnings multiple of five, reviews a company with pretax earnings of $3 million, interest expense of $400,000, and bank debt of $5 million. The multiple of the earnings before interest and taxes produces a $17 million purchase price: subtract the $5 million debt (if the buyer is to assume it), and the financial buyer is willing to pay $12 million.

If you are selling the stock of a corporation, the buyer will receive any excess cash. Such cash should be added to the earnings multiple to arrive at the price. If your business has excess cash of $2 million, pretax earnings of $3 million, and the negotiated multiple of pretax earnings is five, then the price should be $17 million.

An ordinary distribution business might sell for about four times the earnings before interest and taxes. An attractive manufacturing business with a record of consistent earnings, good margins, and good, but not superior, prospects, could expect to command, from a financial buyer, a price of five to six times the earnings before interest and taxes. Special circumstances lead to variations.

In ebullient times, when buyers are tripping over themselves to find sellers, and funding is abundant, financial buyers might stretch to eight times the earnings before interest and taxes. You will know when the climate is this favorable: it is rare, and it will be discussed in the newspapers. The norm for financial buyers, especially for deals under $30 million, is around five times the earnings before interest and taxes–and these are "adjusted" earnings, after adding back expenses that would not continue for a new owner (see page 124).

If one customer accounts for 20% or more of a company's sales, this tends to decrease the price, as does a lack of management depth, and weak trends.

Factors which aid a higher multiple include high depreciation (or other non-cash charges to the income statement) versus required capital expenditures, so that a buyer could expect "free cash flow" in excess of the income on the statement. Also key is the profit margin–if earnings before interest and taxes average about 8% of sales in your industry, but your business earns 14% of sales, then you can seek a premium. Proprietary technology and products, large market share, barriers against others entering your business, and, of course, superior prospects all help to command a higher price.

Assumption of Debt

Misunderstandings occur–and sometimes survive through several weeks of talks–regarding assumption of debt. The buyer, especially a financial buyer, is likely to expect you to pay off any debt from the proceeds of the sale. You may have a different understanding.

When you agree to sell the assets of a business, the buyer usually takes over the payables and other current liabilities. Bank debt is seldom assumed when the buyer is acquiring the assets. If you agree to sell the assets of your business for $10 million, and the business owes a bank $3 million, you might expect to walk away with $10 million, except for taxes. The buyer might expect you to pay off the $3 million bank debt from the $10 million. Clarify this point, *before* you discuss a price. And, of course, know if you are discussing the sale of the stock, or the assets, before you discuss a price (see page 126).

Strategic Buyer

Strategic buyers *can afford* to pay you more, because they can expect economies not available to other buyers. So why doesn't everyone sell to a strategic buyer? They are, quite simply, in short supply.

Strategic buyers, moreover, pose different risks: they might take longer to close (processing deals is not their principal activity, as it is for financial buyers); and they operate in your industry–where leaks of talks might hurt you in the market. Unscrupulous or not, they might, without buying your business, acquire and exploit your confidential information.

And some strategic buyers are not willing to pay any more than a financial buyer. Some executives reason that if their resources can help your business, that is not something they expect to pay for. Furthermore, a strategic buyer is likely to understand your business well, and confronted with the prospect of paying, say, three times the value of your assets, an executive might begin to wonder how your operation might be replicated, perhaps for a much smaller sum. It would, of course, take a long time, but your business lacks the element of mystery, the allure of something new, exotic, or unknown.

The appeal of innovative technology is a prime example of what can attract a strategic buyer, but how many can claim this attribute? On the other hand, a declining business might appeal to a competitor, and this strategic buyer might merely want to close your operation and acquire your customers.

> It is far better to pick a strategic buyer . . .
>
> –RON MARSILIO, page 48

Proof of the shortage of strategic buyers is in the business news almost every day: financial buyers are completing transactions aggregating in the billions every year. These firms would be out of business if there were enough strategic buyers, paying premium prices, to go around. (Financial buyers become strategic acquirers only when they are adding to a business they already own.)

So catch a strategic buyer if you can, but you may need *two* to get the price up, and be careful with your sensitive information.

Size

Businesses with $5 million or more in operating income are in more demand than smaller ones, and more financing options are available for these transactions. As a business gets larger it has more momentum and more management depth: the risks for a new owner diminish as the size increases. You cannot price a business with sales of $5 million based on the amount paid for a similar business with $50 million in sales.

Price-Earnings Ratio

Buyers of private companies talk of the price in relation to earnings *before interest and taxes.* Stock market tables and investment professionals refer to price-earnings ratios using *after-tax* earnings–an important distinction. The price-earnings ratio of a public company is a reflection of its expected earnings growth rate. Get all the data you can on public companies in your industry. Their investor relations departments will often send out securities analysts' reports on the company and the industry to those asking to be on their mailing list. Know what price-earnings ratios are in this industry, and gain some appreciation of why differences occur. If your company has lower profit margins and is much smaller than a public company in the same business, you will *not* have a good case for the same price-earnings multiple.

> I keyed our asking price to the S&P Industrials price-earnings ratio, which at the time was in the neighborhood of 15 or 16 times earnings. That's an after-tax multiple . . .
>
> —JIM SCHILL, page 64

Purchase Accounting

Accounting rules prescribe how a buyer records the purchase of your business—and they can affect the price. Purchase Accounting rules apply to almost all transactions—those with private companies, financial buyers, foreign buyers (with rare exceptions), and even public companies if they buy for cash.

To apply Purchase Accounting, an appraisal is made of the fair market value of the individual assets acquired. The aggregate of the market values is then subtracted from the price paid for the business, and the difference is goodwill. This goodwill has to be written off or go on the balance sheet of the buyer. Goodwill is unattractive on a balance sheet: bankers and creditors disregard such intangible assets, or even deduct it from the equity to establish the tangible net worth. It gets worse: buyers are required to amortize goodwill over at least 15 years, and deduct these noncash charges from income. The buyer records the income from your business only from the date of the acquisition under Purchase Accounting.

Look at a suitor's balance sheet to see if it has goodwill. Footnotes should explain the origin. No goodwill suggests that in the past this company has avoided paying high prices in cash transactions (or written off the goodwill at the outset).

Selling to a Public Company

Public companies worship growth: it drives their stock prices, their price-earnings ratios, and the income of their executives. If you have products, markets, or technology coveted by public companies (and you should know this if you do your homework), as well as a growth rate of 15% or better, your target, if you want the best price, should be a public company (U.S. or foreign).

If the stock of the buyer is selling for thirty times its after-tax earnings, then *theoretically* it could afford to offer (in stock, see below) this multiple to you without diluting its earnings per share, a critical measure for public companies. Nevertheless, even if your earnings growth rate matches or exceeds that of the buyer, its executives may not be willing to put your earnings on the same plane as theirs. And accounting rules play a role.

Tax-Free Exchange

Nirvana for many sellers is being acquired by a *successful* public company in exchange for its stock. Generally such transactions are tax-free (you pay tax if you sell the stock) if many technical requirements are met. You should have qualified professional help to guide you (ask about "step-up" in basis at your death and the lower taxes your heirs may face). All your equity in one stock is not ideal, but you do have liquidity if the company is large enough. You could sell some of the stock for diversification, and pay the associated taxes.

> We sold for stock the first time in 1972, and it had some unforeseen consequences when the stock price collapsed a year or two later, but we took the advice of our advisor and we sold 25% of the stock we received within a week of the merger.
>
> That was Ken Leventhal's advice. That was our book value, and then we could ride on the house. If anyone merged with a company in exchange for stock, I would recommend that they secure the same right: do it, and hope it is the worst sale they ever make—because they will be riding with 75% of the acquisition price in stock. But if it goes down, then they haven't been blasted.
>
> —Mayer Mitchell, page 32

Pooling-of-Interests

If you sell your business for common stock in the acquiring company, it may qualify for "pooling-of-interests" accounting treatment. Intricate rules (best explained by your accountant) apply: the key benefit is that the buyer does not have to write off any goodwill. When a transaction qualifies for pooling-of-interests accounting treatment, your assets and liabilities are recorded on the buyer's financial statements without any adjustments: if the price is five times your book value, this disparity is not apparent anywhere on the books of the buyer–no goodwill on the balance sheet, and no amortization of goodwill. This is an important advantage, and may mean a higher price.

If the buyer treats the transaction as a pooling-of-interests, the buyer's income statements, for periods prior to the acquisition, are restated to include the results of your business, to make it look as if the buyer had owned your business in earlier years. If your business represents a noticeable share of the two together, expect a careful analysis of this restatement to see if the trends of the combined businesses are favorable.

Be sure to understand any restrictions on your right to sell shares. Some buyers might propose to give you unregistered stock, and SEC rules can limit your ability to sell shares quickly. The rules for a pooling-of-interests also restrict stock sales. If the shares are thinly traded, you probably cannot sell a block without depressing the price. You may need a formal, underwritten secondary offering of your shares to get out–something to negotiate with the buyer before the closing. A deal for shares loses its appeal if the liquidity is questionable, unless you willingly lock up your position and have great faith in the success of the buyer.

British Accounting

To avoid goodwill, the next best thing to a pooling-of-interests is to sell to a British company. Changes are being discussed, but British accounting rules in 1997 do not require the amortization of goodwill on the income statement. A British company that buys a business for $10 million over its asset values can write this off against its retained earnings. It is not painless, but the sacred cow of professional managers is earnings per share, and this number is unaffected. This may seem remote from your concerns, but it can have a direct bearing on how much a buyer is willing to pay.

Tease?

It takes months to buy a business. An offer without the appropriate study is just a tease–and financial buyers are more promiscuous with such offers than public companies. A non-binding offer from someone ill-informed about your business is hollow.

Competitive Buyers

> Have at least two buyers. It takes their mind away from, "Gee, are we sure we want to do this?" Instead they think, "Gee, I hope the other guy doesn't get it." In that mind set, the buyer is a lot easier to deal with, and to move along more quickly."
>
> –Ron Marsilio, page 48

Best is two or more strong parties who have studied and want the business, and now face some competition when they address the price. Two covetous buyers can inflate the price magically.

But you face a predicament. You work hard, and suffer disruption, to get just one party to know enough about your business to make a serious offer. You have little inclination to try to get someone else to the same point. Months later, you may wish you had.

Terms and Conditions

A buyer might jokingly say, "You can name the price, if I can state the terms." Think about that. You may be able to get a higher price if you offer seller financing, but is that an acceptable risk?

The price is not the whole story. It is not only when you get paid, but what representations and warranties you are asked to give. Are you going to be vulnerable to a claim of breach of warranty?

Take your time when price is being discussed, especially if you have more than one suitor. Get a sense of the price each would be willing to pay; and get a sense of how onerous their definitive agreement–their terms and conditions–would be (ask to see one they have used before with the names blocked out). Is an offer "subject to financing?" If so, how speculative is the financing?

> You can accept a lower price if you have a better structure.
>
> –JONATHAN DILL, page 50

Purchase Price Adjustments

Definitive agreements often provide for purchase price adjustments to be made some months after the closing. The buyer might want to reduce the price by the amount of any shortfall from a guaranteed net worth (or net working capital) at the closing date. You might ask for the reciprocal adjustment if there is an excess.

For a public company selling a division, the recording of a profit on the sale can be as important as the price. So it will often fix the price in relation to the net assets of the business being sold–for example, the price might be a $3 million premium over the net asset values. After the closing, accountants will determine the net asset values as of that date, and a price adjustment will be made.

If you are selling the assets of your business, carefully analyze the difference between selling for a fixed price, say $10 million, versus selling for a fixed premium over your net assets, say $4 million over net asset values on the day of closing. Inventory and Receivables can fluctuate in unanticipated ways, and these adjustments can bite you.

And think about the profits to be earned between the time of the agreement in principle and the closing–are they to accrue for the benefit of the buyer or the seller? They should be yours, but a buyer might propose price adjustments that take them out of your pocket.

Valuations

Some firms provide valuations, primarily for estate purposes and for Employee Stock Ownership Plans. A written report will address valuation from various viewpoints–discounting the expected future cash flows, addressing values of individual assets, and comparing your business with others reported sold in the recent past and extrapolating from that pricing. If you produce such a valuation for a buyer, don't expect it to be a cornerstone for negotiations (but it can be helpful to a financial buyer who wants to estimate how much a bank would lend on your assets). Future cash flows are uncertain. All businesses have unique characteristics, and finding comparable transactions is a stretch. Look at stock tables–often two seemingly very similar businesses, say two big banks, sell at very different price-earnings multiples. Perceptions of management, and other intangibles, defy measurement–except by supply and demand. Getting two or more bidders to make offers for your company will price it like nothing else.

Relative Strength

Buyers will judge your performance versus your competitors. Profit margins are the measure. If your pretax profits margins exceed 10% of sales, you are ahead of the average for all American businesses. If your pretax margins are 12–14%, or higher, and the aggregate profits are over $1 million, buyers will line up to talk to you. How do your margins compare with those of your competitors?

State an Asking Price?

Some buyers refuse to visit a company without first knowing an asking price. Pitch it too high, and you kill off the visit. Pitch it too low and you lose. Do enough homework to give a range, and to discourage bargain-hunters. If your business is worth a maximum of five times earnings to most people, and you state you want eight times, you may not get much attention. Don't drive away good buyers with an outlandish asking price. The object at the outset is to attract suitors.

> It is important, I think, that you get away from the business, with a third party, to price it. When you own something, you always think it is worth a lot more than outsiders happen to think it is worth.
>
> –A. J. LANE, page 16

But you could say you want six times the adjusted pretax earnings–that leaves room for arguing about the appropriate adjustments, and you might negotiate for six times the earnings in the twelve months preceding the closing rather than six times the earnings in your most recent fiscal year–or, if business is booming, you might suggest six times the adjusted earnings for the *current* fiscal year, with provision for some price adjustments after the year is completed (and a monthly budget for the current year will bolster your case).

If it is clear that you are going to be talking to several buyers at about the same time, to see what they might offer, you could say you think the business will sell for $40-50 million, but you are not sure. If two or three are interested at around $50 million, you might be able to get $53 million. That would be understood by all, and you would not have lost anything by starting at $40-50 million.

But often the circumstances are quite different. You are entering talks with a qualified buyer, and you don't have anyone else interested–and you don't want to search for a competitive suitor. You don't want to reach too far on the price and drive away your one buyer, and you don't want to leave money on the table. This is a time to be vague. You want to draw this suitor in, provide information, and let the executives of this company ruminate about the benefits of owning your business. You just provide information in the best possible light.

Think ahead. If pressed for a price, you want to state one that will allow for some movement. You might state a price of $22 million. The buyer listens to the rationale for that, and offers $18 million. Then, if the parties want to make a deal, there will have to be movement on both sides–and $20 million now looks logical. Picking an asking price about 10% above the high end of the "market" range has merit.

> If you are really and truly prepared to walk away, I believe you'll get a much better price.
>
> –Greg Smith, page 85

Holdback

If you are selling at book value, or a price close to the market value of the assets, you should not have to discuss a holdback. If the price is five times the book value, and you do not have audited financial statements, the buyer can make a strong case that it would be fair to holdback, or put in escrow, 10–20% of the price, for, say, two years. If there are no breaches of representations or warranties, these funds should be released on schedule. Sometimes the release is tied to no loss of key customers, revenues, or profits. Your nightmare is a false claim, and litigation. It happens. Hence the importance of homework on who you are dealing with, and how they have dealt with others.

> In our experience, and I have compared notes with others who have been through similar experiences, buyers often count on getting that escrow money back through indemnification claims.
>
> –James Hackney, page 82

Little or No Profits

If a multiple of earnings is not more than the market value of your assets, you should seek a deal based on asset values. Book value is a norm widely used as a price for businesses with low earnings. Cash for 100% of the price is still your ideal, but that might be unrealistic. Helping the buyer could lead to a higher price. You might (1) keep the Receivables–the buyer could collect them on your behalf; (2) lease the real estate (and perhaps the machinery and equipment) to the buyer; or (3), in extreme straits, retain ownership of the inventory, and let the acquirer buy it from you as it is used.

Withholding Information

Most businesses have warts. If some toxic chemical was dumped behind your plant a few years ago, you are better off disclosing it–and other likely problems–before the price is agreed. You don't want to negotiate the price more than once–you are in a stronger position the first time. If negative news comes up later, the seller might reassess the price. Worse, if the bad news shakes the buyer, the deal can founder–as the buyer's executives wonder what else you are not disclosing, and they lose confidence in your integrity.

Assume competence. The buyer, and its army of lawyers and accountants, is likely to uncover problems before the closing. You are better off identifying the problems rather than letting them be discovered.

> The buyer is always asking himself what is there about this used car that he is not telling me. Why are you selling this if this is such a good deal?
>
> –Michael Mintz, page 14

Earn-Outs

Earn-outs bridge credibility gaps. This is an increment in the price withheld by the buyer and paid only if the business earns targeted profits in one to five years following the closing. They can create many difficulties–in negotiations and in practice. Some buyers will not entertain earn-outs because they cause conflicts of interest–the seller is more interested in the earn-out than the general welfare of the buying company, and the managers involved feel they are on different teams. Negotiating the ground rules either cuts corners or is painfully detailed: you could specify in detail the accounting rules to apply, or you could just say the same as used before.

You may need the buyer's capital to finance the growth expected in the earn-out period–are you to be charged for this? On what basis? And what of the risks? The buyer must retain discretion about how much more capital to put into the business–and buyer and seller may see the risks differently. The seller might claim the earn-out would have been achieved if only the buyer had provided more capital. But sellers have incentives–their earn-outs–to take risks they would not take with their own money.

The buyer acquires the prerogatives of ownership at the closing, but, in an earn-out, is expected to surrender some of them temporarily–an unnatural, and often uncomfortable, circumstance. A key one is the right to make management changes.

In theory, if a business is thriving, the buyer wins big as the seller achieves the earn-out, and so is unlikely to starve the business for capital, or interfere in the management. In practice, unexpected circumstances develop, personnel change, and conflicts can fester.

The details are endless. Is the earn-out all or nothing? If you achieve 40% of the target, do you get 40% of the reward? (Usually not.) You might get part of the reward for achieving 90% of the target. And what if you make the target easily two out of three years, but miss it in one year–are the rewards based on cumulative results? (Some could be, but a public company is rewarded for smooth, steady growth, and sellers are, too.)

How much of the price should be in an earn-out? Some offer a seller a chance to earn 100% more than the initial payment over five years, but much more common is a chance to earn 10–30% more over one to two years.

> Each buyer looked at the company differently. One said, "Let me take you over, and you can earn more than just the purchase price." But that's a big mistake. When you sell to someone else, you give up the right to manage. If they take the business down the tubes, then the benefits they offered off in the future never materialize.
>
> You may sell to less than the highest bidder if someone offers a sweetheart futuristic deal. Now you have turned management over to them. They don't do the things that you would do. The things you had in mind for growth don't happen. Now all they have to do is refer to the contract and say, "Well, this didn't happen, therefore. . . ." And it's the end of the story.
>
> Buyers are, with all due respect, bullshittters. I would recommend that you get the price that you need and want–anything on top of it is fine.
>
> –Robert Perfetto, page 79

Bottom Line

The ultimate yardstick for an offer is, compared to what? Compared to keeping the business, or the odds of finding a better offer. Someone around you will inevitably say an offer is inadequate—often it is flattery, or an attempt to discourage you from selling.

Judgment is a key to your business success. When an offer comes in at a price somewhat shy of your target, your judgment will be tested. Ardor can be ephemeral. If you do not act promptly, the buyer may move on. You will have to rely on your instincts, and your knowledge of the market. The advice you receive is only as good as the source—and no one else has the stake you have.

> . . . deals take place when each side thinks they are getting more than they are giving . . .
>
> —RICHARD MCCLELLAN, page 20

13
Negotiations

Read *Getting to Yes: Negotiating Agreement Without Giving In* by Roger Fisher and William Ury of the Harvard Negotiation Project. This short book, a paperback published by Penguin Books, is a perennial best seller. Also read *Smart Negotiating: How to Make Good Deals in the Real World* by James C. Freund, an attorney with a wealth of experience in large mergers and acquisitions. He also wrote *Anatomy of a Merger,* which provides invaluable insights into the key role of lawyers and the nuances of negotiating definitive agreements.

All research emphasizes one point: the ultimate weapon of a successful negotiator is a good alternative–another suitor, or no sale. Skillful use of this option, apparent or real, is the challenge.

> . . . you probably have to walk away from negotiations once . . .
>
> –RICHARD McCLELLAN, page 20

Everyone stresses, properly, the value of having several parties interested. The reality of many business sales, however, is that you have only one party seriously interested, and you're trying to complete a deal with this one company.

Early Skirmishes

From the first meeting, you are wondering how much the buyer would be willing to pay, but the buyer is thinking about what it would be like to own this business–what might it be in five years? You need patience. Bragging about other suitors can hurt your cause: it takes months to buy a business, and no one wants to waste time. Buyers, husbanding their resources, look for reasons, like an unrealistic price or a highly competitive chase, to cull a deal off their list.

But you do want to discourage bargain hunters. A broker acting as gatekeeper can limit visitors to those with interest at a threshold price level. If you think it is reasonable to expect at least six times the earnings before interest and taxes, you can instruct the broker to limit visitors to those willing to contemplate this price.

Mediocre Record

When past results are mixed, margins are mediocre, and the outlook unclear, the early contacts should encourage a buyer to visit. You hope to coax the buyer into seeing the benefits of owning the business. Defer the discussion of price. You want the hook to set, before you pull.

Listen

The process takes too long, and too many people are involved, for pure salesmanship to clinch a deal. Selling too hard can raise suspicions. Listening skills are key: most buyers will reveal why they are interested in your business, and, armed with this information, you can help them *persuade themselves* of the merits of the acquisition.

> Pick someone in the company as a confidant.
>
> –James Robinson, page 72

Strong entrepreneurs often want to deal alone with a buyer: they have all the votes, and they don't manage by committee. When you are concentrating on those points you want to get across, however, you may not listen well, missing significant signals. Take along a trusted associate to listen and observe, and you will have a valuable resource to review the meeting when it's over.

Scout

The first meeting is likely to be with a scout. Titles vary, but the job of this person is to screen acquisition opportunities. The scout gathers enough information to write a memo for colleagues describing the opportunity. You will be asked about your price expectation so that it can be mentioned in the memo. If the reaction to the memo is favorable, the buyer will bring other more senior executives, probably line managers, to a second meeting.

Decision-Maker?

You make your own decisions. You want to deal with your counterpart. It seldom works that way. The buyer's CEO is unlikely to handle the negotiations. Consensus management is common in big companies. Accept that their decisions take longer than yours.

Venue

The buyer's office is not ideal for price negotiations. You may be uncomfortable in the unfamiliar surroundings, and you may be facing new people. An executive might try to demonstrate to colleagues tough negotiating skills. It is worthwhile to visit the buyer's office, but try to do it before price negotiations.

Sponsor

Someone in the buyer's organization is the sponsor, the prime mover promoting the merits of your business. This person wants to make the deal–and is in many ways your ally. Review contentious issues with this ally privately as much as possible. Don't let problems be uncovered by accountants or lawyers and travel along different communication channels. When problems arise with others, call on the sponsor to participate in the discussion.

Try to negotiate the price informally with the sponsor. The sponsor will know what they can offer. You can steer your position to the outer edge of what they will accept. The sponsor may not be able to commit at that instant, but might be willing to take up your case and present it to colleagues as "what it takes to get the deal."

> Meet with your counterpart in the other company and forge an agreement with him, so that the spirit of the agreement carries through when the attorneys and others start nit-picking.
>
> —JACK MCCHORD, page 63

If, on the other hand, you try to improve the deal after receiving a written offer from the buyer, it is harder to change. People have taken positions. Executives for the buyer want to be tough, not wimps. They don't want their colleagues to think that you can manipulate them.

> The way the seller interfaces with the buyer is critical. It is difficult to sell a business on the telephone. When you get down to finalizing a deal, it is best done in person. Stay in the room until the deal is locked up, and then you shake hands and walk out. Trying to deal via fax machines, and on the telephone, takes out the personalities. Credibility can be questioned. Little things can become big things. And they should be resolved immediately—or they just fester.
>
> —SCOTT BROWN, page 109

Getting Around to Price

> They figured . . . you ask one price, but you are willing to accept a lower price. They kept coming back, and we kept saying, "No, we are not interested. Get lost. That's the price." It took them about a year to understand that we were serious.
>
> —JONATHAN DILL, page 50

Buyers might make their first offer at 30% below their view of the market price. It is the only way to find out what you might take. The best will make you feel that this is their final offer. Here is where you need fortitude. The buyer who walked away last week may come back this week with a better offer. And this can happen more than once. If you hold out in one of these exchanges, and it turns out that the buyer does not come back, you could, after a suitable pause of a week or two, offer to reopen talks at a lower number. A go-between is useful for such signals.

Don't Rush to Get It in Writing

Sellers like to get an offer in writing. It seems more real. This is a milestone they have been seeking for some time. *This is not ideal.* The trouble with an offer in writing is that it comes with a space at the bottom for you to sign, indicating your agreement. And the clock starts running. Most offers have a time limit of about two weeks. The letter making the offer spells out more than the price: it has accompanying terms and conditions. You may not like some of them. Worse, the letter is not legally binding–it says so. Yet the buyer wants part of it to be binding–the requirement that you stop talking to other buyers.

> If the individual selling can possibly do it, I would slow down the process. There is a lot given up just in timing–"we've got to do this, we've got to do that." The next thing you know, you've given away a million dollars. Part of that is sometimes guys get to the point when they are apart–whether it is one dollar or a million dollars–where somebody will inevitably say, "Let's split the difference." If you are going to split the difference, let the other guy tell you that. So that he has already come up half-way, then you have the advantage of being able to say, "I can't quite do that–but if you toss in another $100,000, we'll do it." So if the gap were one million dollars, now you've got $600,000 instead of $500,000. Pace is important.
>
> –Woody Comstock, page 60

Friendly, but Not Too Friendly

A natural reaction to being courted by executives from a larger organization is to show warmth and enthusiasm for an association. Both sides strive to establish rapport. Keep at a polite distance. Keep them guessing. When they make proposals, take time to mull them over.

Curb your desire to get on with it. Let them know in a day or two (not weeks). A delayed response might be better than an instantaneous one. Don't think aloud with them. Signaling your enthusiasm for a deal prematurely could be expensive. You can be friendly without signaling that the buyer has a "done deal."

Ask

A proposal is made, and it is okay, but you would really like to sweeten it. Ask. Don't demand. You may still want to make the deal even if you cannot win these points. It is remarkably effective to tell the sponsor what you want: this is best done informally, perhaps over lunch or dinner, not in a room full of people. The buyer wants you to be happy with the deal. The sponsor can urge colleagues to accommodate you.

> In negotiations, you can't be afraid to ask.
>
> —Don Joslyn, page 100

Don't react impulsively to an offer. It's best to mull over the concessions you want, and to plan a strategy. If you ask for three concessions at once, the buyer may concede the least consequential one in an effort to appease you, and not move on the other issues. Ask questions about how they established their position, and this should allow you to probe for concessions. The buyer may have based its proposal on some erroneous, or excessively conservative, assumptions: you should try to open a dialogue on the underlying issues, and it should become apparent if there is room to improve the offer. Once you have pressed the key issue, usually the price, to the apparent limit, you can request other changes.

> . . . I was much too quick to accept what they offered . . .
>
> —Sam Newington, page 89

Brokers can float trial balloons, and ask for concessions. If there is an impasse in price negotiations, they can try to patch together a compromise—at a time when buyer and seller are both reluctant to initiate a phone call, not wanting to be the first party to cave in. But brokers have egos and their own ideas: you should carefully manage their participation.

> . . . the buyer actually wants a win-win, if he is going to keep the people.
>
> –EDWARD YOHMAN, page 37

Buyer's Style

Negotiations can be simple and short, or tiresome and take a year. As you compare competitive buyers, you must make some assessment of their style–would they exasperate you by dissecting every issue, or would they breeze through focusing only on the broad issues? If you have two equally qualified buyers interested at around the same price, discussing a draft of a definitive agreement with each of them will quickly show their stripes.

> One's initial feelings about the people you are going to be negotiating with would tell you which category they are in.
>
> –KEN POORMAN, page 43

No Script

You cannot write a script for your negotiating strategy. Much of the time you are reacting. Unexpected events occur, as in "One Story" in the Appendix (page 222).

The best negotiators can put themselves in the shoes of the other party and see the critical issues from that viewpoint. With this perspective, you are better able to choose where to push and where to compromise.

Some negotiators love to posture. They make erudite speeches explaining, like a professor, why the value of your company in today's market is not a penny more than five times the pretax earnings. Keep in mind they may also make similar speeches explaining why a business is worth 15 times the pretax earnings when *they* are selling. Do not try to match the eloquence. Listen impassively, and keep them guessing about your options.

Battle Scars

You don't want to impair relationships with future associates. Be a listener in some negotiating sessions. You might want to fight hard on some points, but you can let a colleague or broker make the arguments: the case for a smaller holdback, and a shorter time for the survival of the representations and warranties. If directly challenged, you could deflect the question, saying you'll not take a position on every point, but are interested in judging the entire transaction as one package.

Momentum

Talks should develop, and maintain, momentum toward a closing. Lose it, and the deal may be in trouble. Buyers constantly reassess the odds of closing. They work intensely on some deals for months, only to have serious business problems uncovered, or, worse, the seller have a change of heart. Buyers develop sharp antennae for signs of trouble. If momentum falters, the buyer may wonder whether the seller is having second thoughts, or perhaps negotiating secretly with someone else.

> If you are just toying with selling, well toy with it by yourself.
>
> –Arthur Hilsinger, page 76

Giving up ownership is, of course, a once-in-a-lifetime decision–but for a buyer the transaction may be routine. The time for the soul-searching is before you start talks with the buyer. Qualified buyers are not easily replaced. When an attractive offer is presented, action must follow, or you could lose the buyer. A buyer has managerial resources devoted to the pursuit of your company, and if it appears you are not ready to sell, the buyer may move on. Once a buyer has "wasted" time on a business, it is very hard to rekindle the interest.

Keep in Touch

The sponsor is managing the buyer's efforts to acquire your company, and closing your deal must become this person's top priority for a while. If it slips to a secondary position, the odds of closing diminish. Maintain contact with this person every two or three days as soon as you think you have a deal. The rapport you develop will be helpful, and you want to keep up with developments at their end. Don't delay answering calls. If you have not spoken for several days, find a reason to call. If they are backing off, you want to know. Remember, they may be seeing a continuous stream of alternative investment opportunities. If you are slow to return calls, or unavailable, they will immediately suspect that you are in negotiations with someone else. Once you have agreement on the price, you want to proceed rapidly.

Buyer Delays

The pace is controlled by the buyer. Except in an auction, a seller cannot tell a buyer when to make an offer, or when to write the check. If the buyer is slow to return calls, or there is no apparent progress being made, it could be a sign of trouble, but there are more people involved in creating papers in the buying organization–including people you will not meet. When they prepare a document to send to you, it might be circulated to a dozen people (specialists in tax, human resources, real estate, insurance, finance, environmental, patent, heads of related operating units, and others) for comments, before they pass it on to you–this takes time. The sponsor will tell you what is going on.

Sometimes, after several weeks of negotiations, you hear that the chief executive, or some other eminent personage from the buyer, wants to visit. Don't be alarmed. It usually signifies that, with the final commitment not far away, the boss wants to confirm that you, indeed, have a good business.

Wait for the Finish Line

Don't drop your guard too early. Having struggled for months to find a buyer at a good price, you may sigh with relief and sign an agreement in principle. But these deals often falter at a later stage. The buyer may demand onerous terms in the definitive agreement, and in this light the price no longer looks so good. Or your pressure on the price has driven the buyer to the edge of his comfort level with the risks, and any bad news in the due diligence tips the scales and the buyer withdraws.

And keep close-mouthed about your intentions with employees and others around you. Telling family and others about progress step-by-step inhibits you from switching plans as you learn more about the buyer. You get unintentionally committed by all the surrounding expectations.

Reassess Your Hand

A realistic, and continuous, assessment of your hand is crucial. Ask too high a price, and some buyers will disappear. Announce an auction, and some will opt out. Seek earnest money, and buyers might grow scarce. Demand your definitive agreement, and you may deter your best-looking buyer.

And early assessments may well be wrong. So many buyers are trolling for acquisitions that you can be misled by the number of people eager to come and see you. Buyers are abundant, but until they see all the details, and you see their price, they are only *lookers*.

14
Letters of Intent

Shut Out Competition

Uppermost in the buyer's mind, if there is competitive interest, is to get your signature on an agreement in principle (usually called a letter of intent). This shuts out the competition. *It also brings to an end your efforts to get a higher price.* Financial buyers do not begin serious analysis of the business, or their financing options, before reaching this milestone.

You, on the other hand, should not rush into this. Before accepting a proposal, you want to develop a sense of what else might be possible—what other suitors might offer. If you have narrowed the field down to two or three serious buyers, your ideal is to coax talks along to the point where the suitors all suggest a price, or offer a letter of intent, within about a week or so of each other, so that you can compare. All you can do to hurry them along is sow fears that they might lose the deal.

Not Binding

Agreements in principle state that they are not legally binding, and they can seem innocuous. Sellers eagerly await this first written commitment by the buyer. It is a *pivotal* moment because it begins events that tie you to this buyer. This is the time you will probably announce the deal to your employees–it is too uncertain before, and it is unlikely you can keep it secret afterward.

Free Option

These letter-agreements usually include a commitment by the seller not to talk to other buyers for a 60- to 90-day period (called a "no shop" clause). The buyer needs this assurance to commit resources to studying the business in detail, the *due diligence.* Something is inherently unfair about this. The buyer does not agree to refrain from talking to other sellers. All the buyer is committed to do is to study the deal–and this can be terminated at any time.

So some attorneys refer disparagingly to agreements in principle as free options. You agree not to negotiate with others for some months, but the buyer is not really bound to proceed. The buyer has an option–and can drop out at will, and lose only the expense incurred in the investigation. The letter of intent states that it is subject to a mutually acceptable definitive agreement. Either side could take an impossible position and kill the deal. It is not secure.

But two months into the due diligence, you are caught. By this time the emotional and other commitments to go ahead are substantial, and if the buyer suddenly lowers the price there is pressure to compromise or give in rather than explain to everyone why it did not close.

You might conclude, however, that it is worth taking two months to try and make a deal–and later you can reassess everything. But two months later you have a better appreciation of all the complications of these deals, and you will be reluctant to cover this ground again, with all the associated disruption of your business, and uncertain outcome, with someone else. (This is especially true if you lack audited financial statements.) You will feel that a closing is perhaps a few weeks away–so, if asked, you grant a request to extend the time. The buyer has you in his web.

Earnest Money

Some sellers demand payment–a non-refundable deposit–in exchange for taking their businesses off the market for a while. It might be $250,000, $500,000 or $1 million. Some buyers, sometimes corporations with sales in the billions, will say they have never paid such earnest money. I would not doubt it. Exercise caution. The object is not to win a non-refundable deposit.

Stigma

A broken deal, a failure to close after an agreement in principle, can be a stigma–for the seller, but not the buyer. Bystanders wonder what problems the buyer found.

Need One?

You could suggest bypassing the letter of intent and proceeding to the definitive agreement. Some buyers will not proceed without a commitment by you to stop talking to other suitors, but others might be willing to forgo the letter of intent and start work immediately on the definitive agreement. You should welcome this approach.

Corporate Buyer versus LBO Firm

A corporate buyer may take longer to propose an agreement in principle than an LBO firm, but it might be more secure. Corporate buyers tend to complete more of their review of the business before entering into an agreement in principle–not the records of the company, but their analysis of the prospects. A corporate buyer may have the marketing or technical experts on their payroll and get their opinions before proposing a price. An LBO firm often hires consultants after they have an agreement in principle.

Financing uncertainties are the biggest bane of proposals from LBO firms. Problems with lenders can lead to a lowering of the price *after* a signed letter of intent.

Not Ideal, but Common

Most deals have an agreement in principle. Sellers like to see the price fixed, and it is progress towards a closing. Buyers also like to have an established accord on the price and key terms, but the buyer has leverage afterward. Some homework could pay off. Talk to principals who have sold to this buyer before, and ask if there were any surprises after the letter of intent was signed. Some buyers will have a more straightforward record than others.

Buyers usually write letters of intent–here they make their offers. Sellers sigh with relief if the price looks right. Everything else looks like boilerplate, and the urge to sign, indicating acceptance, without consulting an attorney, is strong. After all, the letter says it is nonbinding.

But now is a good time to win key points–a time when the buyer is afraid you might turn around and talk to others. If you can, discuss the terms of the agreement in principle orally–then you will have a better chance to influence its content. The ideal would be to agree on a price, and then have attorneys for both sides negotiate over the words in the written document. Bring up some of the major terms of the definitive agreement. *This might gain you some extra time to await an alternative offer.*

15
Lawyers

Comparison Shopping

Shop for a lawyer–and learn. This is a critical choice. The wrong one could cost you a deal, or leave you vulnerable to litigation. You need a practiced specialist, but there is no shortage, and they do not have to be in your city or state. Offer to visit their offices and you will have more choices than if you ask them to come to you. The visits will be well worth the time invested. Bankers, accountants, friends, brokers, could all be sources of leads to attorneys for you to interview. They might go to a friend (or someone who refers business to *them*), but you can judge for yourself. If you cannot find lawyers with appropriate depth of experience in negotiated acquisitions, look for the largest or best law firm in any commercial center: here you are most likely to find people with the right expertise.

Beware of the rainmaker: many firms have an impressive person who signs up the clients, and the work is then farmed out to others to perform. Ask to meet the person who would be negotiating with the lawyers on the other side in *your* deal. Would this lawyer command respect?

> Get a good lawyer. Not just a garden variety neighborhood lawyer . . .
>
> –David Halpern, page 92

Fees

These transaction fees will be higher than any you have incurred before. A $4 million deal might incur legal costs of $45,000. A $40 million deal might result in legal fees of over $200,000. In theory, the costs are not related to the size of the transaction. The expense will be bearable if the deal closes (and the buyer might even pay). If it does not close, the expense will vex you, but fees are more negotiable than you might expect.

> I would try to negotiate a price up front with the lawyers. If you leave it open, the pricing is based not on the hours spent but on the perceived value to the seller. When you go to the broker you know pretty much what it is going to cost you, but when you go into the legal system–unless it is negotiated up front–the price can vary pretty widely.
>
> –Art Bollinger, page 33

Same Objective?

Leveraged buyout firms, conscious of transaction costs and the frequency of fruitless efforts, ask their lawyers to put a cap on the legal fees for an acquisition. They also negotiate a different fee schedule for ones that do not close–a law firm might bill at 50–80% of its normal rate for a broken deal. These are not cut-rate or second-class lawyers. At the *outset,* discuss ways to controls these costs. Your bargaining power will be hindered because you are not likely to be a source of repeat business. Moreover, your inexperience could make you put more demands on the time of a lawyer, and thereby drive up costs. You can, however, find a lawyer willing to work efficiently, and to link fees to the outcome. Top law firms are making it known that they are willing to be "creative" (read *negotiate*). Sharing the same objective, a completed deal, is a *decided plus.*

When to Start the Meter

When first to consult an attorney? Spending an hour with an experienced lawyer early in your deliberations would alert you to key issues.

Do not sign a letter of intent without experienced legal advice. Even if you have no alternative buyers, and are delighted to get an offer, you can still win some points. You may be in no position to dictate terms to the purchaser, but you can push gently for changes. But you need a lawyer to help.

> The price is critically tied to the terms.
>
> —Bill Cash, page 57

Now is the time to make sure that other terms besides the price are acceptable. The buyer might propose in the letter of intent that there will be the usual representations and warranties, covenants, and escrows. It could mean 5% of the price tied up in escrow for one year, or 25% tied up (and perhaps never released) for three years. The economic stakes are high. The terms might facilitate the buyer suing you for millions.

For you, the more of the details that are negotiated and spelled out, the better. The buyer wants to delay some of these difficult discussions until later, when you are more committed to the deal (and competitive buyers have long since moved on).

Negotiating Strategy

Dozens of issues have to be negotiated in these transactions. Some are vitally important, and some are minutiae. It costs money to do legal battle on all these fronts, and you should have a voice in assessing the cost versus the benefit. Discuss a budget for the legal work, in hours and dollars, with each lawyer you interview, and get some understanding of their approach to the contract negotiations.

Paying your lawyer to draft agreements favorable to you may be fantasy if the buyer has quite different views. Assess your hand carefully.

Lawyers often like to control the negotiations, but their ethical codes limit their actions–your lawyer has to communicate via the buyer's lawyer. And the best route to solving a problem might be lunch with an executive of the buyer.

> One of the things I had said to the buyer was "Let's make sure that the lawyers simply put down what we agree to." But lawyers are not wont to do that–lawyers are being retained by somebody, and they always feel that they have to give that somebody an edge.
>
> –Jim Schill, page 64

Style and Egos

Some people like their attorneys to function like attack dogs. The buyer looks at your lawyer as part of your team, and a reflection of your style. You want to protect your position, but you do not want to be labeled impossible to deal with. Develop a clear demarcation in your mind between legal and business decisions–and make sure you make the latter. When they overlap, as they do, those decisions are yours. You *must* exercise control over the negotiations.

Tensions can develop between the legal teams. Personalities play a role, and you have a bigger economic stake in the outcome than any of the attorneys. Remember who is paying the bills. You want to keep apprised of the climate, and you can do this by having an associate, perhaps your financial officer, attend meetings of lawyers.

> Use your own good discretion in dealing with lawyers. Have the lawyers keep you from getting into legal problems. Most lawyers are on somewhat of an ego trip. They get into these things, and they think it is like a big game–and they want to win. They want ups on everybody. I wanted to get rid of the business. I used to get on the phone to my attorney and say, "Phil, don't blow this thing. I want out, and I want out now. I am willing to give in on that point and this point." He had a hard time giving in.
>
> –Ken West, page 35

16
Due Diligence

The buyer's executives want to be able to look back and establish—in court if necessary—that they exercised all the reasonable care in the purchase of your business required of someone with a fiduciary responsibility, someone investing other people's money. This is the due diligence, and it begins as soon as you have an agreement in principle.

> . . . go through a preliminary due diligence on your own.
>
> –Ron Marsilio, page 48

Now you are in no-man's-land. The deal is tentative, but the buyer starts presuming certain rights. Buyers expect freedom to talk to employees and to learn everything about the company. Employees' allegiances may start to glide over to the buyer, as they anticipate the new power structure. The buyer feels the deal is there for the taking, but has no obligation to go forward. You don't have a solid deal, and you have agreed not to look for one with anyone else.

Confidentiality Agreement

The buyer probably signed a confidentiality agreement before your first meeting, months before this stage. It was one thing to provide information on paper about your company, and to conduct a tour of your facilities, but now the buyer is going to have access to much more detail, every detail. Perhaps your original confidentiality agreement needs bolstering. Think ahead, and require new undertakings about confidentiality as part of the agreement in principle.

Subterfuge

A buyer planning to rely on other people's money arranges the financing during the due diligence period. Prior to an agreement in principle, banks and other financing sources do not study the transaction in any detail: at this time the price is unsure, and the buyer might lose the deal to someone else. Delays may be attributed to the due diligence, but they may be caused by financing problems.

Financial Statements

The buyer starts with the financial statements. If you have audited statements, the buyer may want to send in other auditors to review their work. If you don't have audited statements, the buyer wants to send in accountants to get as close as possible to such numbers–and this can take months. The absence of audits prolongs the due diligence. The buyer's accountants have questions. Your employees now know what's going on.

Bankers

Bankers often visit soon after an agreement in principle. Once again you will find yourself selling. Financial buyers may bring equity investors to see your business. During such meetings you may wonder if you knew enough about the financing plans *before* you signed the agreement in principle.

Consultants

Some buyers will bring in management or marketing consultants to write a report on your standing in the market. This can lead to rumors. Many people are involved now, and leaks occur.

Environmental Issues

No buyer, or lender, is going to accept unknown liabilities associated with environmental problems. Every due diligence checklist highlights environmental assessments. Specialist firms will check all the appropriate government agencies to see if you have been cited for transgressions, and they may suggest test wells to look for water pollution around your facility.

Contracts and Company Records

The buyer's lawyers will want to see all your significant contracts–with customers, suppliers, landlord, etc. And they will want to review minutes of all board meetings.

> We had established the price, and we had even established the time. It looked like it was going to take four months to put it all together. And I mean it was just brutal–you could not imagine. Our people would say, "Why do they keep asking the same questions over and over and over?" They would ask the same question to half a dozen different people, and then they would send somebody new in to ask the same questions. It was check, and double-check. And then at the time when we thought everything was finished, that the due diligence was over, then the attorneys came in. And the attorneys started all over again. They looked at it all from a legal standpoint, but the scrutiny of the paper trail was still incredible.
>
> –FRANK HUBBARD, page 101

Full Disclosure

Tell the buyer everything: it is in your interest. You have come this far, you want the deal to close. Problems that arise late can unnerve the buyer–and lead to questions about the price, the business, or your integrity. These can kill a deal.

Signals

Watch the buyer's spending. If a buyer decides to withdraw, action will follow promptly to cut off further expense. Auditors leave, or there is a strange silence as the questions stop and the buyer mulls over the difficult call to you. These expenses can run into the hundreds of thousands for travel, consultants, lawyers, and accountants. The more they spend, the more reluctant they are to withdraw. Executives of financial buyers can be penalized in their paychecks by broken-deal costs.

Extension?

Provide answers quickly when questions arise. Your best interests are served by minimizing the time required for due diligence. Your accounting staff will be overloaded at this time, but you should make it clear that answering the due diligence questions is a top priority.

> Respond quickly.
>
> —Jim Cullen, page 26

Many sellers routinely grant an extension of time for the due diligence. This is a time to step back, and make a new assessment. Now you will know the buyer much better than you did when you signed the letter of intent, and some weaknesses may be apparent. You will have had a chance to see whether their plans are well conceived, or weak. You will know if their execution of plans is a strong suit, or lacking. You will have seen their proposed definitive agreement, and will have had some negotiations about it. You will feel wedded to this buyer by the intense activities of the preceding 60 days—but do not routinely grant a time extension. Their failure to meet the time schedule may mean trouble with their financing, and you should carefully evaluate the reasons for the delay.

If you are dealing with a public company, you might feel insulated from these due diligence uncertainties because your letter of intent is not subject to financing. Your letter of intent, however, undoubtedly states that the transaction is subject to a mutually acceptable definitive agreement and approval by the respective boards of directors. Public companies often proceed beyond a letter of intent, only to withdraw later because they could not get board approval. The reason may be totally unrelated to your business: a common one is for the board to say the buyer's management should solve some internal problems before acquiring any more companies.

Now you will be glad you kept your finger on the pulse of the deal by regular communications with the buyer's team, even if you had to contrive reasons. You should have learned exactly where the deal stood in the (financing or management) approval process, and its progress step-by-step. You will pick up concern if problems loom.

If you decline to grant the extension, the buyer might terminate efforts to buy your business, or may be willing to continue even though you may now talk to alternative buyers. A seller starting to have some doubts about the buyer might refuse the extension, but agree to continue negotiations. This puts pressure on the buyer–and it may be appropriate, unless you were the clear cause of delays.

How strong are your options? This will be the question. If the business is thriving, if you had other anxious suitors when you signed the letter of intent, and if you have lost enthusiasm for the original buyer, refusing to grant a time extension could be a welcome way out. If your business has weakened, and this is slowing the buyer's progress, then you should perhaps control your pique and help the buyer to get it done, even if more time is needed. During the due diligence, assess your options, and the buyer, *continually.*

17
Definitive Agreements

These agreements are the terrain of properly trained and experienced lawyers. Your guidance must come from your carefully chosen professionals. Here are some of the issues you will face.

First Draft

Receipt of the first draft of the definitive agreement marks the beginning of a protracted, tedious, but crucial stage of the negotiations. It usually lasts several weeks. Staying power, even obstinacy, can help.

Attorneys will advise you of the merits of preparing the first draft of this agreement. If your hand is strong enough, and you are running an auction, you can make the rules: you can give suitors your draft of a definitive agreement, and ask for comments.

Most sellers are not in this position. They have narrowed the field down to one chosen buyer. It has been a struggle, but they have reached agreement on a price–now comes the paperwork. They want to keep the legal bills down. The buyer, who has completed many acquisitions, offers to draft the agreement. The seller acquiesces. More often than not, the buyer proposes the first version of the definitive agreement–this is in effect a more detailed offer. The more of the overall agreement you have established in the letter of intent, the better off you'll be when discussing the final contract.

Representations and Warranties

The buyer wants you to guarantee that you have disclosed all relevant information about the business, and that the presentation of the facts, in particular the financial statements, has been fair. If not, the buyer wants to be able to withhold payments owed to you–or to sue you. This can get contentious. You suggest, that after all the due diligence, the buyer's team knows more about the business than anyone, and it should rely on its own investigation. It sounds good to you, but it is unlikely to prevail. If there are disputes after the closing, the representations and warranties in the agreement will get close scrutiny. A buyer paying a full price is likely to look for strong guarantees. Now you might be glad you invested in audited financial statements. It is harder for a buyer to quarrel with the fairness of financial statements if they were audited.

> Watch your reps and warranties.
>
> –Jack McChord, page 63

Your lawyer will negotiate a "basket." You don't want the buyer making numerous small claims due to alleged breaches of representations and warranties. A basket of $50,000 would mean that the buyer can make no claims against you unless in the aggregate they exceed this number–and then you may be responsible for the total, or perhaps just the excess over the $50,000 basket.

Indemnification

The buyer is going to ask you to provide indemnification–against losses caused by breaches of representations and warranties, undisclosed liabilities, fraud, and perhaps other events. The amount of this indemnification is a major issue. Some buyers say it should be unlimited, on principle. Some sellers say it cannot exceed the price, or perhaps the after-tax proceeds. In essence, it is a function of negotiation and price–a buyer paying a great premium over asset values is likely to seek more indemnification than one paying book value; and a seller with a back-up buyer can stand firm.

Holdback

The buyer might propose that part of the price (15-20% is often used) be set aside, and held back or put in escrow in a bank for a year or two, so that claims can be made against this pool before the funds are released to you. You will get interest on this money, but it will be at risk for a while. This is one reason to continue managing the business: if you are a key manager, the buyer will not want to jeopardize the relationship with you–and your relationships with key customers–by withholding releases of escrow funds (unless there were egregious misrepresentations). You want to minimize the time the funds are held in escrow. You can argue that all the buyer needs is about six months beyond the time of the first full audit of the business under new ownership.

Some escrows might be tied to retaining a certain level of business, especially if the buyer is afraid of losing some key customers. If the buyer ties this to sales volume, you should suggest no penalty if you achieve the targeted earnings even if sales fall below the agreed level–and you might propose to have the test based on an average of two years, so that you can make up any shortfall in the following year.

Give Something, Get Something

You cannot expect to win every argument concerning the definitive agreement. Cooperation and progress are required. Look at the whole picture–if you are being beaten down repeatedly, maybe you should reserve judgment on some key issues, and put them on a list. Later you can give in on some, and insist on winning others.

Sometimes a buyer absolutely has to win one point. The CEO, the board of directors–someone–has decreed a certain holdback, or something, is essential. The issue is a *deal-breaker*. You hate to give in on this point, but you step back and look at the whole picture, and the overall deal is still one you want to make. Concede, if you have to, but make them pay for it–get something in return. The best way to extract a concession is in exchange for something they want.

> You have got to yield on some things if you expect to get anything back.
>
> –DAVID HALPERN, page 92

Employment Agreements

The privileges of ownership include the right to change management at any time, regardless of employment agreements–but with a contract you would still be paid if you are replaced or shunted aside. One year after the closing it is common for buyer and seller to work out a new settlement, with the seller giving up management.

The buyer wants the employment agreement in part to prevent you from competing with the business you have sold. Ask your lawyer what courts have found to be unenforceable in these noncompete agreements: you should not be bullied into signing something that no court would find to be reasonable. But beware of fighting too hard here. If the buyer suspects that you might later compete with the business you are selling, you can imagine the reaction. Let your lawyer handle these negotiations.

Arbitration

> I am very happy we had an arbitration clause in the agreements.
>
> –JAMES HACKNEY, page 82

You must provide for disputes. Newspapers tell us frequently of the deficiencies of the courts–the expense, the delays, and sometimes surprising verdicts. Large corporations turn often to "Alternative Dispute Resolution." Retired judges sometimes act as arbitrators, and firms have been created to offer these services. Some contracts provide that disputes will be settled by *binding* arbitration under the rules of the American Arbitration Association. Ask your attorney about this. When you shop for your lawyer, discuss this subject, so that you can get more than one professional opinion on this important subject.

Small Print

> Everything should be detailed in your written agreement–go over it once, and then go over it three, four, or five times before you say that it is final.
>
> –DAVID HALPERN, page 92

Make sure everything you have agreed to is in the documents. You know the business better than your lawyer, and you should catch problems that others would miss. Do not delegate this agreement entirely to your attorney. Ask your accountant to read a draft of the agreement. In a large corporation, at least half a dozen people would review a definitive agreement. Don't let your concern about secrecy deprive you of valuable suggestions from others.

> Looking back, I would take further advantage of counsel to understand some things that perhaps I didn't have a real clear concept of at the time. There are certain formulae involved that are tied to the performance . . . for me at the time, I thought I understood, but very honestly my understanding was not as clear as it should have been.
>
> –JACK PARLOG, page 54

18
Buyer Lowers the Price

Let Down

You have an agreement in principle to sell for $12 million in cash. The buyer has been arranging financing and performing due diligence for eight weeks, and makes an appointment to see you. The buyer's accountants disagree with the way you have treated certain entries, and they think last year's income was overstated by $350,000 (a similar discussion can arise from a reduced estimate of the current year's income). Their price was based on six times the earnings before interest and taxes, and now they propose to reduce the price by six times $350,000, or $2.1 million. What triggered the price change–new information, or new views about the *right* price?

White-knuckle time. Perhaps you will wish that you had not told so many of your family and friends about the pending sale. Try to understand the reasons for the change. Have investors, or the bank, declared the price excessive? Much leaks out because there are so many people involved. Now you will be rewarded for good communications–you should know the key milestones: getting commitments from investors, or approval from the board, or for a bank loan. Try to find out what triggered the price change.

Emotions can boil to the surface when a trusted buyer drops the price. You might feel cheated, betrayed, or manipulated. You want to tell them they acted badly–or worse. *Be careful.* This buyer had a strong initial interest. This step may have been forced on them by a superior you've never met, or a banker, or an investor. It may be a ploy. They may want to go ahead at the original price if this move fails. There is only one way they can find out if you would go ahead at a price 20% below that in the letter of intent. And they have to appear to mean it. Restrain yourself: don't say things you might regret. They may come back and offer 5% below the original price, and you may want to accept that.

Now you will be happy if you've told the buyer that other suitors exist. (Don't mention names–the unknown are more threatening.) You must let them know you have acceptable options. You will be happy if you have taken steps to minimize the feeling among your employees that the deal is a foregone conclusion.

How to Respond

Your answer to the new proposal is that you need time to think about it. Take at least a week. If they want the deal, they will begin to sweat–and you will see signs. Someone will call you. Perhaps a go-between seeking information on their behalf–it could be a lawyer or an accountant. Tell them to stop the due diligence, and remove their people. If you have another strong buyer, you could ask for all your confidential papers to be returned–but do not play this card lightly. Alternative buyers will present new uncertainties, and your best outcome might still lie with the original suitor.

How valid is their reason for reducing the price? This is relevant. If you have just lost a customer who represented 40% of your business, they have a point. But if it is something that has no bearing on future profits, then they may not.

If you conclude that you still want to try to make a deal with this buyer, take several days to think about it. Then ask if there is room for negotiation. Some point between their new price and the original price may seem like a logical place to compromise.

Alternative Buyer

Recognize that attrition rates are high for acquisition talks, and keep friendly with all those seriously interested in the business. Before talks founder, you may sense that trouble lies ahead. The buyer is expressing concern about the quality of earnings, or the prospects for the business. You feel you're being prepared for a price reduction.

Now it would be nice to know how the other buyer you spurned a month or two earlier would deal with the issues that have arisen. Find out if you can (and a broker can do this more readily than you) how aggressively interested they are in your business. Some buyers will take the position that you should finish your talks with the first party before they will get involved. Others will sense an opportunity, and readily jump in and try to be competitive. Do not rely on what they said a month or two earlier. Then they might have been pursuing another company, and were therefore preoccupied.

Providing data is key. The second buyer is not going to be able to address price and other issues without all the information. Your letter of intent may preclude "talks" or "negotiations" with others–this is a good reason to have provided data to more than one buyer before entering into a letter of intent.

The seller in "One Story" in the Appendix had an agreement in principle. He also had an alternative buyer. He kept sending the monthly financial statements to the alternative buyer, and kept them apprised of where he stood. He was not negotiating with them: he was keeping them warm. When the first deal fell apart, he was able to switch to the second buyer easily.

If your first buyer is now suggesting a deal different from that outlined in the letter of intent, your obligations not to talk to anyone else are over, void. The week or so you take to mull over a lowered price is an excellent time to have talks with an alternative buyer. This works best when the alternative buyer has visited you before you signed an agreement in principle.

Switching buyers is an emotional wrench for many sellers—and surreptitious talks feel unseemly. Do not succumb to the temptation to brag about a second buyer: if the alternative talks turn out to be fruitless, you'll be weakened. But leaks occur, and may help. If the first buyer still wants the deal, plans to drop the price may be tempered. Keeping other suitors in reserve, and acting promptly if the terms of the letter of intent have been breached by delay or change, is the best protection against price changes.

19
After the Closing

Continuous Negotiations

Negotiations do not end at the closing. Escrow accounts, employment agreements, earn-outs, and everyday operating decisions can all lead to continuing negotiations. It is a different world when someone else owns your business. You may miss the perquisites of ownership. The happiest sellers are those who can adapt. Don't fight unnecessary battles, and accept that the new regime is going to have its way–in accounting systems, budgeting, personnel policies, capital expenditures, and most other things.

But you can rule again: some rare sellers go on to take over the management of the acquiring company.

What They Want from You

Ideally, you will find an interesting role in the new organization. And often most appealing is a chance to try to initiate other acquisitions. For many buyers, your ability to introduce them to new acquisition opportunities may be *your most valuable contribution*–more important to them than your ideas (they have their own) about how to run the business. Use your industry relationships to help the new owner locate additional acquisition opportunities. You might enjoy being on the other side.

Buy It Back

Acquisitions frequently fail to meet the expectations of buyers. Expectations are often unrealistically rosy. They seldom anticipate downturns in business. When they inevitably occur, it can lead to a reassessment of the business by the new owner. Management changes may occur at the buyer, and may lead to a revised corporate strategy: your business may now be peripheral to the new goals. Look for telltale signs. Have relationships deteriorated? Are they no longer concerned about keeping you motivated? How do they refer to your business in their annual report?

Don't leave too abruptly. If the relationships have become poisonous, that may be tempting. They may be forcing you to make decisions you know to be unwise. And they may not allow you to take steps that would help the business. Going to work is torture. And you can afford to stay at home.

Look past the immediate frustrations. An opportunity may be looming. Successful businesses usually sell for many times the book value. A poor performing business being shucked off by a public company is often sold for book value. And it gets better. If the sale of the business to anyone but you would be troublesome, the seller might finance much of the transaction. Don't empty your desk too soon. You might be able to make *two* winning transactions.

APPENDIX

Resources

You can review vast amounts of business information using your computer. Here are some suggestions. If you experiment, you will find many more sources of online information. As with all intelligence gathering, you have to sift. You might have to look at 15 or 115 articles to find one that is right on target.

Internet

Entire books, entire shelves, can tell you more about the Internet. I shall give some examples of how it can be useful.

Listservs

To learn more about publishing, I joined the Publishers Marketing Association, a trade group for small publishers. For two years I scanned its monthly newsletter, and learned from some of the articles. One day I read that it was going to set up a Listserv e-mail forum (also known as a *mailing list)* on the Internet, and it gave an address. The advantage of a Listserv is that it is entirely based on e-mail. I followed simple instructions to join the list by sending an e-mail message to an address provided. Hundreds of others interested and active in publishing have done the same. Participants send an e-mail message to the Listserv when the mood strikes them, and everyone on the list gets that e-mail message. It might be a question, or it might be a statement. Others then answer or comment. A subject that attracts several messages becomes known as a *thread*, and it is enlightening to hear several knowledgeable opinions on the one topic. Messages fly back and forth about problems and opportunities in printing, distribution, legal issues, marketing, publicity, computer topics, and other items of interest to publishers. I have learned one hundred times more from this than I ever did from reading the associated newsletter. To participate, I just open my e-mail account at a time of my choosing, and retrieve all my messages.

This group sometimes exchanges 100 messages in a day, and to save expense it is best to use a command that downloads all your mail as fast as possible, so that you can read it off-line–America Online, CompuServe, and other services offer this capability of reading mail with no meter running. Once off-line, you can (with word processing software) review the subject line of each message, and read only those of interest to you. The information is right up to date, and a peer group is commenting on the merits of positions taken. Often the value is a reference to another source–a vendor, a book, or a newsletter.

Look at industry and trade association publications in your field, and watch for announcements of a Listserv on the Internet for participants in your business. Discussion groups on the Internet take other forms, too–thousands of USENET newsgroups share views on every conceivable topic. Dialogue on a Listserv is likely to be more focused than on a newsgroup, and participants are more likely to have a long-term commitment to the subject.

You can search for Listserv e-mail forums by sending a message to this Internet address: Listserv@Listserv.net. In the body of the message you place the command LIST GLOBAL /DENTISTRY, if dentistry is your interest. The search is for key words, and even if the title of the Listserv is an acronym, the search should identify forums that include words in the full title. Alternatively, you can go to an Internet website, http://www.liszt.com, and search for such forums.

Another example. My wife has an unusual autoimmune disorder. A newsletter of a patient support group announced a Listserv e-mail forum for those with this condition. Now a group of over 200 people from various countries exchanges messages on medications, developments, and other news of interest to these patients. A professor of medicine in Holland, a specialist in this condition, suggested a precise dosage of a medication for my wife on this Internet Listserv, and her local doctor gave her the prescription. Communications like this on the Internet, among people with *very specific, common interests*, are bound to grow enormously. Such contacts can be an invaluable tool–and could help your business to grow. You might find new customers, and better ways to serve those you have.

Search Engines

If you want to look for information on the Internet's worldwide web on any conceivable topic you need software to find what you seeking. Such software devices are called *search engines*, and one of the most useful is that of Digital Equipment Corporation, called *Altavista.* You can search for a word, like *modem*–and you can choose advanced search and look for *modem* and *Hayes*–and refine it further by searching for *modem* and *Hayes* not *external.* You go to Altavista by accessing this address, http://www.altavista.digital.com. Altavista could help you find a website for a particular company. Other leading search engines are http://www.lycos.com and http://www.yahoo.com–and Internet browsers offer a broad choice of search engines. Use of these tools is free.

Mergers and Acquisitions Internet Site

Buyers and sellers of businesses can leave messages for one another at an Internet site, M&A Marketplace (www.mergernetwork.com). Brokers seem to be the most frequent users of this site. For sellers it is perhaps *too public*–but your company could be described here by a broker, or someone else acting on your behalf.

SEC Filings

The annual reports that companies file with the SEC are called 10-K's, and they often provide a more comprehensive business description than that found in the annual report to shareholders. Quarterly reports filed with the SEC are called 10-Q's, and they often have more information than the quarterly report to shareholders (10-Q's include a section titled "Management's Discussion and Analysis of Financial Condition and Results of Operations"–this information is not always in the quarterly report to shareholders).

Unusual events, like acquisitions, are reported to the SEC on reports called 8-K's. They are filed at the end of the month in question–but are not required if the acquisition (or other event) is small in relation to the size of the reporting company. If you are in serious negotiations, check to see if the buyer has reported any recent 8-K's: you might find in this SEC filing a complete definitive agreement used in a prior acquisition, and this might prove particularly useful.

Two free Internet sites, http://www.networth.galt.com and http://www.stocksmart.com, offer summary financial data and stock price information on any public company, and they provide links that allow you to print the SEC filings of the companies you select. And if you are looking for information on a public company that is traded on Nasdaq, you could go to the Nasdaq Internet site, http://www.Nasdaq.com, and enter the symbol of the company in question on the quotes page–there you can click on an icon that will take you to the SEC's site, and you can print out the company's SEC reports. You can go directly to the SEC's Edgar Internet site at http://www.sec.gov/, but it is more cumbersome than the other three sites.

Websites of Publications

You might want to search all available sources for information on a particular company or subject–and, besides using the top Internet search engines, you might review the Internet sites of leading business publications. The *Wall Street Journal* has a site at http://www.wsj.com (you have to pay for membership and searches here); *Business Week* has a site at http://businessweek.com; and *Fortune* has a site at http://fortune.com.

CompuServe

CompuServe (1-800-336-6823) provides many services, including access to databases assembled by others. It is widely used by those seeking business information. Some of the data available via this online service can also be found elsewhere (for example, on Dow Jones News Retrieval).

Knowledge Index

Dialog is an information services company with one of the most comprehensive collections of online data available anywhere. It is, for example, widely used by librarians. It can be expensive to use, especially if you are not skilled in its use. Dialog and other similar services can be accessed on CompuServe by typing GO IQuest.

Much data, such as magazine articles and news releases, are available via a dozen or more computer services. For some the choice is influenced by the cost. And when the cost is moderate, you are likely to use it more–and experimentation is essential if you are to take full advantage of this resource. Via CompuServe, you can access dozens of Dialog databases at much reduced rates in off-peak hours–after 6 p.m., and on weekends. The off-peak service of Dialog is called Knowledge Index–from CompuServe, you type KI at the GO command. Here you can mine much business information at modest cost. Instead of paying a few dollars per article, as you have to on some services, you pay a flat fee of $20+ per hour (on top of the standard CompuServe rates), and this permits you to get hundreds of pages of information for less than $20.

Public companies issue press releases regularly about earnings and other important developments. Many of these announcements are not printed, or are compressed, by leading newspapers if the companies are small. But you might be very interested in seeing *all* the announcements made in recent years by a company interested in buying your business. You can do this online. First, have the ticker symbol ready before you go online (if you cannot find it easily, go to CompuServe Bascompany (GO Bascompany) and there you can enter the name of the company and get a quick snapshot of information, including its ticker symbol (and a recent stock price).

Once in Knowledge Index, you have a choice to proceed using menus or commands. Using menus, you select business information, and then you choose a database. Most companies issue their press releases via the BusinessWire or the PR Newswire. The BusinessWire database is Busi5 if you use commands, and the PR Newswire database is Busi6. The bane of online information is a surfeit. Experienced users learn how best to limit their inquiries. You can limit them to a single month or year, or take the ten most recent.

Regional newspapers often run profiles of local businesses, both private and public companies. Check the Business Dateline database (GO Busi7 using commands) on Knowledge Index to see if there are articles about the company of interest to you. This database includes over 100 regional business publications–and a profile written a few years earlier could still be of interest to you.

Also in Knowledge Index you can choose the Standard & Poor's Corporate Descriptions database for all public companies (Corp3 using commands) and here you will see a description of the business, its outstanding securities, past results, and ownership of large blocks of its stock. If you check Standard & Poor's News database (Corp1 using commands) you will see the latest earnings reports, and other significant developments.

Another useful Standard & Poor's database is the one with directory listings for over 55,000 companies, including almost all U.S. public companies. It is called the Standard & Poor's Register (using commands, you specify Corp6). Here you can search for all companies in a given SIC code; you can search for all companies that mention injection molding (or anything else) in their business description; you can search for all references to a name (like Gates, or Buffett, for example); or you can search by state, city, area code, or other attributes, and combinations of attributes. You can specify all companies with given characteristics and sales over $50 million, but under $900 million—or other limits. Buyers use this and other similar databases (such as those of Dun & Bradstreet) to identify their targets. This is available on Knowledge Index, and via other services.

ABI/Inform is another database available on Knowledge Index (GO Busi1 using commands), and the way to explore its contents is to experiment.

If, for example, you are a supplier to Caterpillar, you might want to identify other similar companies. You could search through ABI/Inform and Business Dateline (Busi1 and Busi7 in Knowledge Index) for any and all articles that mention the words "Caterpillar" *and* "supplier" (you can use "suppl?" to include *supply* and *supplier* or any other words beginning with that stem). This search is likely to produce a number of names of companies that supply Caterpillar.

Here (in ABI/Inform) I also found articles by experts on the complex rules that govern the limited use of a net operating loss if there is a change of ownership of a business (I searched for articles including "change in control" *and* "net operating loss").

If you are contemplating selling your business in exchange for stock in a public company, you might be interested in ways to hedge your position in this one stock, and yet avoid triggering taxes by a conventional sale of the shares. Experts write about these strategies in articles found via ABI/Inform: search for "stock concentration risk management strategies" and you should see an article discussing the options, including *equity swap into index of basket of publicly traded stocks*, *short-against-the-box combined with margin loan and call overlay*, *protective put*, and other extraordinary steps that may be beyond the expertise of all but the most proficient and specialized accountants and lawyers.

To gain an appreciation of the requirements and restrictions related to tax-free exchanges of stock and pooling-of-interests accounting treatment, search in ABI/Inform for articles that mention "pooling" and "SEC" and "Rule 144" and "tax-free."

Executive News Service

CompuServe offers Executive News Service (ENS) for a small incremental fee per month. This permits you to have an electronic clipping service–automatically grabbing items of interest to you from major news wires here and overseas. (The *Wall Street Journal's* Internet website offers a similar service, but it does not cover as many wire services.) If, for example, Sun Microsystems is an important customer of yours, you could set up this service to pick up, and save for perusal at your leisure, all news releases that mention Sun Microsystems. You can choose one or all of some 20 news wires (if you are interested in U.S. companies only, choose three–Dow Jones, BusinessWire, and PR Newswire–and you would catch almost all of them). Dow Jones often summarizes announcements, but BusinessWire and the PR Newswire usually include the full text issued by the company. British announcements are often on the PA Newswire, and Reuters has other foreign business news.

Public companies account for most of these news releases, but private companies make announcements, too, especially of new products. A particularly good time to have this working for you would be at the time of an industry convention, when many companies might be making announcements about new products.

You are not limited to company names. If you make modems, or mowers, you could set the system to search for all items that mention modem? or mower?–or any other word or phrase. You can have more than one "folder." So one could pick up stories about your business, and another one could pick up stories about three or four companies that have expressed interest in your business. This will of course pick up some stories of no interest to you, but you can readily scan the results–you have a choice of scanning just the headlines, or scanning the first sentence of each story. Then you choose which ones to read in full.

This electronic clipping service is an *excellent*, economic way to stay current with developments in narrowly defined fields. It is more efficient than scanning newspapers, and it picks up many items that would not appear in the newspapers you read. Software is available that would instruct your computer to dial up this service automatically every hour (or every 15 minutes) to check for news on specified companies or topics. For most people checking it once a day at a time of their choosing would be most convenient.

IQuest

IQuest permits you to access a great variety of databases, to locate newspaper articles or other materials. If, for example, you heard that a British company had made an acquisition of a cosmetics company in a given year, you could enter IQuest and find the *Financial Times* database–and then search the database for the company name, the word *cosmetics*, and the year in question. There you should find the news item, perhaps including the price paid.

Using IQuest you can search for articles on a given subject in dozens of newspapers.

Standard & Poor's

Standard & Poor's "tear sheets" are an excellent source if you are looking for a quick snapshot of information about a public company. You can find them in many public libraries, and sometimes you can get a free sample from Standard & Poor's (try calling 1-800-546-0300).

Abbreviated versions are available online through CompuServe (GO S&P), and other services.

Directory of Corporate Affiliations

This directory, available in libraries, will reveal all the subsidiaries or divisions owned by a large corporation, and it is useful if you are trying to find out if a particular business is owned by another company. This data is available online via CompuServe (GO Affiliations).

Dun & Bradstreet

Dun & Bradstreet (D&B) has many databases you might find useful. They are widely used by buyers (and brokers) looking for businesses in certain activities. D&B's Million Dollar Directory is available on CD-ROM, and this is in many public libraries: often you can download the information on to a disk. So you could go to a library and look up all the companies in one or more SIC codes, with sales in a given range, specify public or privately owned, or both, and go home with a list of a few hundred companies on your disk. It provides only basic information like sales and management background, address, and telephone number, but it is enough to initiate contact.

Applying the same criteria to create a list from D&B, and one from the Standard & Poor's Register, yields surprisingly different names, so if you want to be thorough and track down all companies with your chosen attributes, you should use both. (U.S. headquarters of foreign companies are, for example, more likely to be found in the D&B data.)

D&B data can help you learn more about a European business. You could access their European directories in a library, or you can get information online via CompuServe, Dow Jones New Retrieval, and other services. On CompuServe, you would go to the European Company Library (GO eurolib) where you can find information on over 2 million European companies.

Disclosure

This service (1-800-638-8241) will send you, for a fee, reports that public companies file with the SEC. It also provides data online (GO disclosure in CompuServe). Federal Filings, Inc. (1-800-487-6166) is a competitor of Disclosure.

Association for Corporate Growth

Would you like to socialize with buyers? Join the Association for Corporate Growth, Inc. (ACG). Active buyers belong to the ACG, and they meet to talk about how best to find and buy companies. It has headquarters at 4350 DiPaolo Center, Suite C, Glenview, Illinois 60025; telephone 847-699-1331. The ACG has chapters all over the country, and they usually have monthly meetings for breakfast, lunch, or dinner, at which a guest speaker makes a presentation about how to be successful making acquisitions, about financing for acquisitions, or some related topic.

Every spring the ACG has an annual convention, usually in Florida or Arizona. It is a three-day event with hundreds of participants from leveraged buyout groups, corporate acquisitions executives, brokers, and various service providers. Buyers expect to hear about sellers from brokers and from corporate executives with divestments to discuss. Prominent acquirers make presentations, and experts discuss the how-to of acquisitions.

You could easily join this organization. If asked, you could say you want to learn how to grow by acquisition. No one would doubt it. They all sing the same tune.

Consider going to the annual meeting. It is billed as a place to network. You do not have to be a member, but it costs a little more if you are not. They would be happy to send you the program. You might find your buyer there.

British Companies

British companies are usually the most active of foreign buyers in the U.S. acquisitions market, and most leading British companies derive a large share of their income from U.S. operations. So you may be looking for information about one or two British companies. If it is not provided to you, you can find it on your own. If the British company is publicly owned, as is likely, pick up the *Financial Times*, the British newspaper printed on pink paper. You will find it in major airports, if it is not readily available in your area. Go to the stock tables and you will find a symbol next to many names indicating that you can send a fax to a number given at the end of the tables and request that the annual report be mailed to you (it does not come from the company in question, but from a central service provider). The *Wall Street Journal* and *Barron's* offer a similar service for U.S. companies.

If you use the electronic clipping service of CompuServe, you could be catching all the news announcements made by this company on the news wires (particularly the PA Newswire).

If you are in protracted discussions with a British company, and you want to read regularly about business and stock market developments in the U.K., you might consider subscribing to the weekly *Investors Chronicle*. Much in here will be of little interest to you, but like any intelligence effort, you have to sift for the few nuggets that count. You can telephone for a subscription at (country code 44)-181-402-8485, or fax (44)-181-402-8490. It costs $200+ for a year.

Business Plan Software

You may not need a business plan for your day-to-day management, but it will be a key document for a buyer evaluating your company. Price is a function of expected future earnings, and your plan is where you tabulate these expectations, and where you provide reasons *why* you anticipate sales and earnings increases.

Business Plan Pro 1.2 published by Palo Alto Software (541-683-6162 or 800 229-7526; fax 541-683-6250) has been favorably reviewed in the small business press, and it costs under $100. You might think a tool used by small companies is not right for you, but what business plan do you have now? This one will arrange data to present professionally to a buyer. It provides suggested text that you can copy, modify, or replace, and it creates charts and graphs easily. Ease of use is its strong suit. If you have no business plan, this could be a vitally important addition to your arsenal as you present your case to buyers.

PlanMaker 2.0 (List Price $129 from PowerSolutions for Business Inc., 1920 S. Broadway, St. Louis, MO 63104; telephone 314-421-0670) is designed to instruct you in the fundamentals of writing business plans, and it has questionnaires on screen to help you. This software, and earlier incarnations, has won kudos in numerous national publications. It includes complete plans that you can customize to fit your business. And it includes tips on how to raise capital, and how to prepare your business for sale. It is designed to help people preparing their first business plan, but produces professional-looking documents. It does not require much computer expertise, and its questions lead you to key issues.

Look also at Plan Write 4.0 for Business (List Price $129 from Business Resource Software Inc. in Austin, Texas; telephone 1-800-423-1228; fax 512-251-4401). This has been highly rated in several publications. It has an integrated spreadsheet program, and a companion product creates marketing plans. The same company offers a software tool for developing and evaluating marketing strategies, and this product is used by hundreds of *Fortune* 500 companies.

□

One Story

This story is not extraordinary, and that is the point. The sale took 18 months; there were agreements in principle with three different parties; and the ultimate buyer blew hot and cold–expressed interest, and then went away for three months; then came back and studied more details, and offered to buy half of the business; subsequently offered to buy 100%, then withdrew again; and then acquired the business.

Two key employees had their own agendas; there were environmental uncertainties; cooperation was required, and unsure, from third parties including the landlord and a government agency; and the health of the business fluctuated during the negotiations.

The business had two similar plants, one in Ireland and one in the United States, and each had sales of $6–7 million. They made commodity components for computer companies. The seller prepared a document describing the business, and it showed profits of less than $500,000.

First Buyer

The owners began by following up on leads they had accumulated, people who had expressed interest in buying the business. This led nowhere, and after six months they asked a broker to help. One of the first companies contacted, a U.S. public company ("PUBLIC") with about $150 million in sales, was immediately interested, and had a senior executive make a contrived "sales" call on the Irish plant within a few days. So much for confidentiality agreements. This suitor produced two pages of questions: their executives were not impressed with some of the answers, and they appeared to lose interest. (They were in fact pursuing another acquisition opportunity with a higher priority.)

Talk to Competitor?

A prime competitor of this business was known to be under pressure from customers to have a European plant, but the seller was reluctant to share data with a competitor. Given the logic of the fit, the seller relented and provided the information. Nothing happened. The competitor had other priorities and problems at that time. (No apparent harm occurred as a result of sharing the data.)

Second Buyer

The broker found a company with complementary, but not competitive, activities–a strategic buyer. It had sales of about $20 million, and it was owned by a leveraged buyout firm. This LBO buyer ("LBO") was interested and, sensing that the seller had few options, offered, by telephone, 70% of book value (around $2 million). The seller was disappointed at the price, but would accept this if all else failed, so a vague response was provided, and there was no contact for three or four weeks. LBO scheduled a visit to the Irish plant for about one month later.

Third Buyer

Now a third buyer, located near the U.S. plant, was interested. It was a company with no knowledge of this business, but it had excess funds, and the principals ("LOCAL") liked to invest locally. They visited, liked what they saw, and produced a written offer within one week. They pressed for an agreement that the seller would terminate talks with other suitors. LOCAL offered about 8% below book value: cash for the U.S. operation, and notes for the weaker Irish business. But LOCAL had not visited the Irish plant. The seller liked these principals, but a non-binding offer based on seeing only one of the plants was flawed. A tentative deal was struck–the first agreement in principle–subject to a visit to the Irish plant the following week. They shook hands and shared some wine.

Now, with LOCAL visiting Ireland, PUBLIC, the one with the initial interest, calls (after a twelve-week silence) to say they would like to buy the Irish plant alone (they can put business into this facility). It is the weaker business, and it should be possible to sell the U.S. plant to someone else, but separating the two would present some complications and additional uncertainties. The seller responds saying this is not ideal.

Now PUBLIC develops more interest and offers, in writing, to buy both businesses for cash at book value. The offer includes an unacceptable provision–the seller has to fire all the employees and allow the buyer to pick and choose among them. (PUBLIC fears the cost of laying people off.) Later they agree to delete this provision.

Government Role

LOCAL is in Ireland, and visits a government agency, one that has advanced funds to the business to encourage training and employment. They are "soft" loans–grants if employment is maintained at a certain level, and technically repayable loans if employment falls. LOCAL learns more about the risks surrounding the weaker Irish business, and becomes frustrated about its inability to lock up the deal and have exclusive negotiations with the seller. LOCAL refuses to offer more than notes for the Irish business–so they could abandon the business at minimal cost if it soured.

The government agency is aware of the various suitors, and it has favorites. It likes PUBLIC because it might be the best for increasing long-term employment in Ireland.

Yet Another Buyer

Another buyer comes on the scene: a second public company that looks like a strategic buyer. They hear that talks are in progress, but they say they can "act like lightning" if they see details and want to go ahead. They visit. Nothing happens. No lightning.

PUBLIC is now pressing for an answer to its written offer, and it has a looming expiration date. The seller wants to understand better what kind of deal could be made with LBO, and, to play for time, offers to visit PUBLIC about one week after the expiration of their offer: PUBLIC's executives are happy to have a meeting on their turf, and they readily agree. Just before meeting PUBLIC, the seller visits LBO.

LBO has discovered that 70% of book value will not get them very far (a competitive buyer has clarified their thinking), so they offer a price equal to book value in cash, with some modest requirements for escrow. Now there is very little separating the offers of PUBLIC and LBO.

PUBLIC has a tendency, already apparent, to be persnickety about details. LBO seems likely to breeze through the due diligence, studying only major issues.

When visiting PUBLIC, the seller is grilled about environmental issues. The U.S. plant is leased. State agency files about prior inspections for environmental problems are missing. A contractor did some remedial work, but a fire has destroyed these papers. PUBLIC makes clear it will not accept any environmental liabilities.

Now PUBLIC decides it wants to study more details before going ahead. It sends auditors to the Irish and U.S. plants. PUBLIC makes several changes in the details of how it proposes to buy the business, and the seller begins to think of dealing with LBO instead. About six months after their first "sales" call, PUBLIC says it expects to sign a letter of intent within 24 hours.

Before the 24 hours are up, PUBLIC decides to withdraw. They say the salary levels in the U.S. business are not compatible with their own, and the U.S. business is less appealing to them than the Irish one.

The seller goes back to LBO. Other interested parties are in the wings, but none are cash buyers. LBO knows what has gone on and decides to exact a penalty–it will go ahead at book value, but as of three months before the closing, and subsequent profits up to the closing (around $200,000) will be for the account of the buyer. LBO says it can close in about 10 weeks.

Three days after withdrawing, PUBLIC calls to ask for more information. Some factions within the company are sorry they have lost the deal, but they reveal they would like to move the U.S. business, and they want the seller to lay off the personnel. This is unacceptable.

Key Employee

The general manager of the U.S. business has a key role, and he makes the presentations when sellers visit. He has an employment contract. LBO wants to hire him, but not have a contract. The seller and the general manager try to work out a cash settlement of the employment agreement, but they cannot agree on terms. The general manager talks of looking for another job.

A buyer with a related business visits, and insists on talking to the general manager alone for a while. He offers him a job. He had little interest in buying the business. The location is undesirable, so it leads nowhere.

Three oil tanks are in the ground at the leased U.S. facility, and they have to be removed. The landlord does not return phone calls. LBO is relaxed–the contract is to state that all environmental issues will be resolved at the expense of the seller.

Business has now improved, and profits are about double what they were when talks began six months earlier. PUBLIC knows that the seller is trying to conclude a deal with LBO, but PUBLIC refuses to express interest at a higher price. The seller has a deal at book value–as prospects improve, this price looks weak, but the seller has no inclination to withdraw from these talks to seek a higher price elsewhere.

Off, Again

Two weeks before the planned closing with LBO, the deal is off. Bankers for LBO went to visit the Irish plant, and the general manager there has unsettled them. The manager did not favor this buyer, and it was not difficult to make the bankers nervous.

Back to the First Buyer

PUBLIC is called, and they are interested–at book value. Their executives refuse to consider a higher price. But it is book value at closing, so it is about 10% higher than the deal with LBO. PUBLIC says it can close in about one month.

The seller had been providing the monthly financial statements to PUBLIC throughout the talks with LBO. They were well aware of the improved financial performance.

Now, a customer representing about 40% of the sales of the U.S. business announces layoffs of tens of thousands of employees, and the closing of a dozen plants. This is a major cloud on the horizon, but it is unclear how it will affect the business. PUBLIC decides to go ahead anyway, and the modest price probably was a factor. The landlord is induced to sign papers acknowledging his responsibilities by the fear of losing a tenant.

The sale to PUBLIC closes after visits by more than a dozen interested parties, and eighteen months after the seller started trying to find a buyer. No one could have anticipated the twists and turns that occurred–and they highlight the need for flexibility, and the pitfalls of relying on one buyer.

Acknowledgments

First, I must thank all those who agreed to be interviewed, and to be quoted. Their advice is the heart of the book.

Several people kindly agreed to read parts of this book, and their comments were invaluable. Some read a sentence or two, and some read it all. I wish to thank Margot Hentoff, Ed Rieckelman, S. Neil Fujita, Paul Boughton, Paul O'Connor, Joe Mack, Dick Bond, Walter Hinrichs, Joan Zomberg, Marvin Levine, Kent Straat, and Theodore A. Rees Cheney–without their guidance, this book would not have been completed.

Glossary

Accretive: A transaction is accretive if it enhances the earnings per share of the acquiring company (usually the result in an exchange of stock of paying a lower multiple of earnings than the price-earnings ratio of the buying company).

Agreement in principle: An outline of the understanding between the parties, including the price and the major terms. It is often referred to as a letter of intent. Usually it is explicitly non-binding, and the agreement is subject to the negotiation of a mutually acceptable Definitive Agreement.

Asset strippers: Buyers who sell some assets of the acquired business, often recouping much of their investment while still retaining ownership of the core activity.

Auction: Inviting bids for a business by a specified date. In practice, the date is often extended for the three or four top bidders, and they are invited to improve their offers.

Audited financial statements: Financial statements that have been examined by independent accountants sufficiently for them to render an opinion on their fairness. Sometimes called certified statements.

Balloon payment: Payment of principal at the end of the term of a note, with no amortization of principal prior to this.

Basket: A designated sum below which claims will not be made for breaches of representations and warranties (or other indemnification claims).

Book: The term used for the memorandum that describes a business for sale.

Book value: *See* Net worth.

Carried interest: An equity position in the buying company provided on favorable terms, or at no cost, to the executives or firm that arranged the transaction.

Comfort letter: Letter provided by independent accountants reporting on financial condition of a company, usually for an interim period since the last audit.

Consideration: Payment. The inducement offered for entering into a contract.

Controlled auction: Inviting selected interested parties to make a proposal, without requiring an offer by a given date.

Covenant: A written undertaking or pledge: examples in this context would be, from the seller, a covenant not to compete with the buyer; and, from the buyer, a covenant in the loan agreement (if there is seller-financing) to maintain the net worth above a certain level.

Deal flow: The number of acquisition opportunities being reviewed by a prospective buyer.

Dilution: If a public company buys a business in exchange for its shares, and the earnings from the acquired company are less *per new share issued* than the earnings per share of the company prior to the acquisition, the transaction is said to cause dilution.

Due diligence: The investigation of a business to assess its problems and prospects to protect the interests of the buyer's shareholders, or those of an institution providing financing.

Earn-out: An increment in the price payable after the closing based on earnings (and/or sales) after the closing.

EBIT: Earnings Before Interest and Taxes.

EBITDA: Earnings Before Interest, Taxes, Depreciation and Amortization.

Equity: *See* Net worth.

ESOP: An Employee Stock Ownership Plan, which allows tax benefits for sellers, lenders, and employees.

Exit strategy: Plan to sell a business.

Fiduciary: A trustee, representing the interests of others, with the associated legal responsibilities to exercise careful judgment.

Financial buyer: A buyer with no strategic reason to buy your business, but one attracted to the financial characteristics of the transaction–usually a buyer relying heavily on borrowed funds to be repaid from the cash flow of the business.

Finder: An intermediary who introduces the parties and performs no other functions.

Flipping: Selling a company within a year or two of buying it.

Free cash flow: The sum of the after-tax earnings and depreciation (and any other amortization, or other non-cash charges to income) less the cash for capital expenditures required to maintain the business. The surplus funds generated by the business.

Goodwill: In an accounting context, this is the part of the price paid for a business in excess of the fair market value of the underlying assets. If applicable, it becomes an intangible asset for the buyer, and is amortized (a deduction from income) over not fewer than 15 years.

Hart-Scott-Rodino Act: Federal antitrust act requires notification of government agencies, prior to closing, of planned business combinations in defined circumstances.

In play: A public company known to be for sale is said to be "in play."

Listserv: An Internet e-mail discussion forum where participants send e-mail to the "list," and all who have registered for the list see each message. Participants register by sending an e-mail message to an address provided by the list manager. Also called mailing lists.

M&A firm: Merger and acquisition consultants.

Mezzanine money: Capital for an acquisition that is more secure than equity, but less secure than debt. An example would be preferred stock with some associated warrants to buy the common stock. This is most often used by leveraged buyout firms.

Net worth: The total assets of a company at their recorded value on the financial statements, less the total recorded liabilities. Also called stockholders' equity, equity, or book value.

No Shop Clause: Agreement to stop discussing the sale of a business to others for a defined period.

Notes: Promissory notes; promises to pay a specified sum, usually to a specified party, at a specified time, with terms and conditions, often called covenants (*see*), in a written agreement.

Pooling-of-interests: Accounting rules that permit a buyer to record on its books the assets and liabilities of the acquired business at their former book value (if the acquisition is made for stock, and other conditions are met). This permits the buyer to avoid recording goodwill (*see*).

Pro Forma financial statement: a restatement designed to show the effects of an assumed change–a financing, a merger, adding back certain expenses; or any other modification.

Prospectus: A Selling Memorandum (*see*).

Pure play: If an acquired company is in one business only, it is a "pure play."

Representations and warranties: Statements made by seller that the buyer relies on (and can be the subject of claims if they are found to be untrue).

Seller-financing: The seller accepts notes (*see*) for part of the price, and thereby lends money to the buyer (or to a new corporation formed by the buyer to purchase the business).

Selling Memorandum: A description of the business, including its history, products, markets, management, facilities, competition, financial statements, product literature, and a review of its prospects.

SIC codes: Standard Industrial Classifications developed by the government which categorize all businesses, and thus allow tabulations of all companies in given activities.

Strategic buyer: A buyer with activities that are complementary to those of the seller.

Index

Boldface numbers indicate principal coverage of a topic.

Order this Book

To order this book, please send $24.95 plus $3 shipping to:

Gwent Press Inc.
14 Darbrook Road
Westport, CT 06880

Or call 1-800-964-1902 to order using a credit card.
Fax: 203-227-9199
Order on the Internet at www.bookzone.com

Contact the Author

Please contact the author if you have comments, corrections, questions, or stories to tell.

Colin Gabriel
P.O. Box 5026
Westport, CT 06881
e-mail: cgabriel@compuserve.com